THE
WOMAN'S
GUIDE TO
FINANCIAL SAVVY

THE WOMAN'S GUIDE TO FINANCIAL SAVVY

by Judith Briles

ST. MARTIN'S PRESS, NEW YORK

To Joyce
And for Shelley
And Sheryl

Acknowledgments

Often the making of a book involves more than an author, and mine is no different, from my husband, John Maling, who encouraged me to finally get it out of my head and onto paper (or at least tape); to Phil Finch who organized it (and me) and pursued us both from deadline to deadline and introduced me to my agent, Jacques de Spoelberch; to Hope Dellon, who edited it with care and good humor and who taught me that one year was short term in the publishing business.

I would also like to thank my staff, who diligently typed, retyped, and typed again each manuscript and its changes: Paulette Henning, Alexis Baker, Charline Deutschman, Shirley Simmons, Marge Hurley, and Yvonne Clinton; and finally, my many friends and clients who participated in the "Name the Book" contest.

Copyright © 1981 by Judith Briles
For information, write: St. Martin's Press,
175 Fifth Avenue, New York, N.Y. 10010
Manufactured in the United States of America

Library of Congress Cataloging in Publication Data

Briles, Judith.
    The woman's guide to financial savvy.

    1. Women—Finance, Personal. I. Title.
HG179.B73   332.024′042   80-28807
ISBN 0-312-88649-7

Design by Nancy Dale Muldoon
10 9 8 7 6 5 4 3 2

CONTENTS

1: The Money Mystique 1
2: Taking Stock of your Assets 9
3: How to Minimize Taxes 20
4: What to Do About Inflation 45
5: Where to Park Your Cash with Interest 57
6: How to Get and Use Credit 72
7: Investments (1): Stocks, Bonds, and Commodities 85
8: Investments (2): Real Estate 131
9: Investments (3): Limited Partnerships 149
10: Planning a Financial Strategy 169
11: When and How to Hire the Experts 183
    APPENDIX I: Net Worth Statement Form 191
    APPENDIX II: Sources of Information 195
    Glossary of Business Terms 201
    Index 213

1

THE MONEY MYSTIQUE

AMERICAN women have changed in recent years. They have been asserting their independence of traditional roles, moving beyond their old boundaries. They have been demanding and exercising their legal rights, establishing careers in fields from which they were virtually excluded just a decade ago.

But the paradoxical fact is that, while women are expanding their potential in almost every other sector of life, a shocking number of them remain woefully uninformed and dependent in perhaps the single most important area of American society.

That area is money. Knowing how to take care of money—how to acquire it, keep it, and put it to work making more money—is an absolutely vital skill for all self-reliant adults, men and women. To be ignorant of money workings is to remain an outsider—a powerless outsider—to an enormously significant aspect of daily life. Without an understanding of what money is and how it can be managed, no woman can expect to be truly in control of her life in this society.

My purpose in writing this book, then, is to share with women some of the expertise and knowledge that I have collected in ten years as a broker, financial counselor, and money manager. In simple and direct language, I want to explain how women can get more money (through financial planning, the smart use of credit, and careful attention to all the legal ways to minimize taxes) and then put that money to work. The aim of all this will be to make the reader better able to evaluate different investments (some of them commonly known, others more exotic) and to use money creatively and effectively—with the ultimate goal of bringing her closer to financial security.

To all the women I meet, I try to stress that financial security is not for just a few. It is not a vague possibility; it is actually within the reach of almost all of us. Many of my clients are working women with salaries in the $15,000 to $25,000 bracket who are paying one-fourth or more of their hard-earned dollars in taxes. They're frustrated and scared because they're seeing their money being eaten away and they feel they're not living as well as they should be on their income. They feel powerless—and it is my job to show them how much power they actually have over their financial situation once they decide to take charge of it.

As a wife and mother, I know personally that struggle to take charge. I remember vividly the incident that impressed upon me the importance of having money and knowing how money can be used. I was ignorant of financial matters when a woman to whom I was very close was divorced by her husband after more than twenty years of marriage. During that time, my friend's understanding of money had consisted of her writing checks to pay bills at the end of each month and then asking her husband to deposit the money in their checking account. Although she and her husband were quite well-off, she knew almost nothing about the family's financial dealings. During the divorce, I saw her pay for that ignorance—which reminded me so much of my own. She lost much of the money that she deserved, was stripped of it, partly by "friends" and family, because she did not know how to protect it and use it to her advantage. I watched all this and resolved that the same thing would never happen to me. I took a job as a secretary in a brokerage house and began to learn, by practical experience, the principles of money management that soon helped me to create a financial strategy.

During that time I started to understand not only how money works but also what it represents. In our society, money is freedom, independence, power. It opens doors that are very difficult to open otherwise. Money represents a choice. You may not wish to live opulently, but at least money gives you the freedom to decide.

Having money can protect you from exploitation of all kinds. One of the first wealthy men I ever knew had made himself a millionaire by his own hard work, expertise, and willingness to take risks. He had gone from literally selling apples and coat hangers on a street corner to a style of life that almost anyone would envy. But then he used his wealth to tyrannize others. When I saw the way he abused the people who depended upon him because of the influence his money gave him, I was even more determined never to be in a position where such a person would have power over me.

Traditionally, women have lacked the information they need to achieve that sort of security. The feeling has persisted that somehow money matters are unfeminine, that women and finance do not mix. Until quite recently, a woman was not likely to be taken seriously when she applied for a loan at a bank. The fact that she was a woman was enough to diminish her credit standing. If she were lucky, she might receive a small "leg loan" because of her looks. For any serious dealings, however, women were considered unfit. I encountered considerable resistance when I began seriously to pursue my goal of financial independence; my family and friends implied and sometimes stated outright that a woman who became actively involved in such pursuits was neglecting her duties as a wife and mother. (The truth is exactly the opposite, for women often find themselves solely responsible for their children's well-being.)

Long before girls grow up to become wives and mothers, parents and teachers tend to discourage them from taking an interest in money and numbers. Until they reach high school, girls are as adept at math as boys their own age, but then it is the boys who are steered toward higher mathematics and business courses.

Even before then, girls are often discouraged from learning

the most elementary financial necessity—the willingness to take risks. In early childhood, scratches and bruises are frowned upon for girls yet somehow considered "manly" for their brothers. The penalties for mischief or petty misbehavior tend to be greater for girls than for boys, who are expected to be somewhat adventurous and daring.

While, fortunately, there are signs that this kind of education for girls is changing, most adult women grew up with this conditioning. I encounter it daily in my clients. Men are almost always more willing than women to invest money in uncertain ventures with high risks but potentially high yields. This puts women at a great disadvantage, since judicious risk taking is an essential element in any successful financial strategy.

The irony is that women need basic financial skills more than anyone, for they are far more likely to be suddenly left alone to care for themselves. Because of divorce or a husband's death, the great majority of women will find themselves responsible at some point for their own financial welfare and perhaps that of their children too. What happens to these women can be tragic. One client of mine, a widow, was tied to a will that compelled her to turn her assets over to a bank trust after her husband's death. This forced her to sell a home worth $250,000 on which she owed a mortgage balance of only $3,000. Undoubtedly her husband never foresaw this extremity, but it happened because he felt she would be unable to handle herself in an emergency and because she never questioned his actions.

The death of a spouse is extremely painful for anyone. But it is catastrophic for a woman who has not prepared herself for the financial responsibility that will be thrust upon her. Because she has never bothered to ask questions about the particulars of her family's finances, she may throw away insurance policies, lose thousands of dollars that could have been saved by prompt action, and suffer terrible erosion of frozen stock accounts until the slow process of documentation is complete.

None of this need happen. Women *are* suited to handling

finance. Housewives and mothers are involved in elementary money management tasks every day, though often they aren't aware of what they are doing because they lack the vocabulary. Balance sheets, income statements, and expense statements are all part of most women's daily lives. The income may be as mundane as a dividend check and a paycheck, and the liabilities as unglamorous as a child's new pair of tennis shoes or the grocery bill for a family gathering. But the basic skills are the same.

Women are good at planning family finances. They may not have known the theory behind their financial maneuvers, but when the tasks they perform instinctively are placed in a context—which is one of the aims of this book—money begins to make sense.

In some cases women may actually have an advantage over men in the money game. They are traditionally expert at shopping and finding bargains, and the same skills that help them to choose the best goods in a market can be applied to the stock exchange. Since they have been shopping and comparing for generations, I try to get my women clients to use what they've learned in looking for an investment. For example, women are in a good position to spot bargains and trends. I teach several classes in investment and money management for women, and one of the questions I ask is how many in the room were aware that coffee was becoming an expensive item a few years ago. Naturally, all of them raise their hands. Then I ask how many used that knowledge to make money. None of them did. Three friends and I, though, pooled our resources, bought a coffee contract on the commodities market, and made more than $70,000 profit in a few months. I knew nothing that millions of other women didn't know about coffee. The difference was that I knew what to do with that information. And once they too have learned how to put their knowledge to work, many of my clients find that the process of choosing an investment is amazingly similar to going into a store and seeing what is disappearing fastest.

Another example: A few summers ago, California was

affected by a statewide drought. Californians were concerned; the subject dominated our lives. Certain well-drilling companies sprouted up quickly, offering people the chance to drill private water wells. For a while those companies were very successful. The drought ended, and most of the companies went bankrupt. While they lasted, though, there was good money to be made if one was able to spot the trend, to take a certain risk, and then to get out at the right time, before the companies began to slide. Housewives all over the state were trying to conserve water every day. They were certainly in a position to spot the trend. But most women wouldn't have known how to invest in those companies, or wouldn't have been willing to take the risk that was necessary, or would have hesitated to sell out while the stock was still healthy.

That, however, is not as true as it used to be. As society's attitudes have changed toward women, so have women begun to change. They are feeling more confident of their abilities, less constrained by the arbitrary limitations that may have held their mothers back. I meet many women in my position as a financial adviser, which puts me in an advantageous spot to sense changes in social attitudes. More and more, I am meeting ambitious young women eager to become aggressive, informed investors. They don't have the fear of money that was prevalent ten years ago. These women—most of them thirty to forty years old—simply want to know how to get it and how to put it to the best use. They are very hungry, and that's exciting. They feel they have been outsiders too long. If they have a fault as investors, it's that they are too eager. They make good investors—in fact, they are often better investors than men—because they are not afraid to admit their ignorance and not ashamed to acknowledge when they have made a mistake. These women learn from their past errors and then are more anxious than ever to start playing the game right.

Interestingly, they are getting a lot of support from other women in the sixty-plus age bracket. These older women realize that they have missed out on something important. They may feel that it's too late for them to change now, too late to become serious investors. But they are full of encouragement for younger women who do want to become knowledgeable, and they are examples of what not to do.

The first thing *to* do is to demolish the mystique of money. There is no mystery to money except that one perpetuated by institutions that feel most comfortable with dependent, unquestioning clients. The sources of information that an investor needs to make intelligent decisions are available to everyone.

One of my clients is a young woman in her late twenties who became the beneficiary of an irrevocable trust several years ago. For her master's thesis she compared the bank that managed her trust with several other banks that managed trusts, evaluating income produced and growth. She discovered that her trust rated lowest not only in growth but also in income produced. The trust had declined 50 percent in value in the four years that she had had it.

My client visited the headquarters of the bank that was in charge of the trust. She met with the managers and told them that she wanted to take control. She was quite confident, she said, that she could do at least as good a job as they had been doing. They resisted her. She got the traditional response: We've been trained to take care of these things; you don't want to deal with problems that you weren't meant to concern yourself with. It is very difficult to "bust," or terminate, an irrevocable trust, but that is exactly what she did. She took the bank to court and ended up with the trust in her own control. And unlike the bank, she has been able to make the trust healthy again.

Few women will be in that position, but with this book I'd like to establish that kind of confidence. I'd like to strip away some of the myths and provide the practical information that a woman needs to begin making her own informed decisions. Sometimes she will need to hire advisers and pay commissions, and sometimes not. (And if not, it's always preferable for her to pay the commission to herself and use it as a reward.) Most of all, like my client with the "irrevocable" trust, every woman should be able to evaluate her financial situation and make sure it is working to her full advantage.

To this end, the advice in this book will be pragmatic and easy to utilize. My own training was practical, which is the best way to learn about money. When I eventually did study for my master's degree and learn the theoretical aspects of this business, I found that my experience gave me a huge advantage over my more sheltered classmates.

A few readers will be intrigued enough by the process of money management to want to pursue a career in investment counseling, as I did. For these women, the time has never been better, the opportunities never more plentiful. Brokerage houses are actively recruiting women for good jobs. And they're discovering that some women are wonderfully suited to this kind of work. My impression is that women tend to be natural salespeople. Especially if they have had children, they have an innate equilibrium, a talent for dealing with problems and emotional upsets. That kind of ability is invaluable in the stock market. Much of financial counseling is simply reassuring the clients, calming their panic at times when panic selling would be a disaster. Women, who have gotten very adept at hand holding over the years, are often superb at that. While the hours are long, especially for junior members of a firm (a forty-hour work week is considered part time), there is much money to be made, and the opportunity is there.

Not all women, of course, will be so taken with money that they will want to make it their career. But each one can and should learn to understand and take control of her own financial destiny.

2

TAKING STOCK OF YOUR ASSETS

For those of us who do not expect to inherit several million dollars from a benevolent relative or who will never hold a grand prize ticket in a sweepstakes or a state lottery—that is to say, for almost all of us—there are no great leaps into immediate financial security. Rather, the process is a series of short steps that begin with the basics.

The first of these is to have a definite goal (or, more likely, several goals) that you want to achieve. These goals ought to be the product of a good deal of thought and consideration. They should not be nebulous or indefinite; they must be clear and articulated. Choosing them is an absolutely personal decision, one that no financial counselor ought to influence. Essentially, it means determining the material circumstances in which you would like to live your life.

We all have our own ideas about that. For one person, it might mean retiring at age fifty and having enough assets to live comfortably ever after. ("Comfortably," of course, has different meanings for different people.) Another person might want to have accumulated a million dollars by age sixty. Others might want to provide education for their children, to travel wherever and whenever they please, to have sufficient capital to be able to invest as they wish in promising ventures. All these goals carry different price tags. You should be able to state specifically what you want and how much it is going to cost, for these factors will influence your financial strategy.

Long-range lifetime goals can be achieved only in increments, so it is important to break the plan down into portions of time that are easier to cope with. You'll want to know what to expect three or five years into the future—and three or five years beyond that. The maxim at the beginning of the chapter is true: There are no great leaps into financial security. Your goals may change from year to year, sometimes even from month to month. Age will also factor in, as well as the ever-changing purchasing power of the dollar. The most important item to stress here is that few of us will have financial security handed to us on a silver platter. The only way to obtain that security is to evaluate your needs and goals and design a financial strategy to meet them.

When you can express clearly just what you want to accomplish, then you're ready to begin. Having established where you want to be, you need to determine where you stand at the moment. As simple as that may sound, I find that few of the people I advise have even a rough estimate the first time they walk into my office.

Besides a copy of their tax return, I require two things of my new clients, and I urge all the students in the classes I teach to provide themselves with the same: an up-to-date credit report and a detailed statement of net worth. You cannot go anywhere without these, since they provide the basic direction and information for your financial planning.

To get a credit rating, you'll need to find out the name of the major credit-reporting company in your own area. You can request a rating in person or by letter. If you've had a negative credit referral within the previous six months, you're probably entitled to get the report free. Otherwise, the charge is minimal—about $4 or $5. It's probably one of the best investments you'll make in your financial career.

A credit report is valuable for two reasons, both of which have to do with the fact that the rating lets you see exactly what a bank or a savings and loan or other lending institution will be seeing when it requests information to evaluate you as a credit risk. You're entitled to this information under the Fair Credit Reporting Act; it's your right to know what is being circulated about you by financial institutions.

Credit, after all, is the backbone of our financial system, and it is definitely a major part of any aggressive financial strategy. To make maximum use of your credit potential in a financial strategy, you need to have a good idea of the extent of your credit. That knowledge will be especially helpful when you begin to assess yourself as a potential investor, which I'll touch on later in the chapter. The point is that you're operating in the dark until you know what kind of financial portrait of yourself is being regurgitated by the computers every time you apply for credit.

But there is another reason, just as valid, for that credit check. In a cover letter that will accompany the report, the reporting company will ask you to notify it if there are any mistakes. The company is required, in turn, to notify anyone to whom it has provided a negative referral on your credit, thus giving you the chance to rectify the mistake. And mistakes do happen. I once found four errors on my own report. Among the mistakes, I discovered that I was listed as having accounts with three different firms with which I was totally unfamiliar. This is serious; a company exploring my credit history might have looked at that information and decided that I already had more credit than I could handle and that I would be unable to meet the overall monthly obligation. So I immediately disputed that information and had it removed.

The secondary elementary step in beginning a financial strategy is determining your own net worth. This is essential, yet, of the students in the adult classes I teach, fewer than half have a decent idea of their own net worth. Of that number, perhaps only another half know how to figure their net worth.

The method is quite simple, once you know what to look for. For that reason, I provide my new clients with a basic net

Sample Credit Profile

CREDIT DATA CORPORATION

Mary Smith
Foster Lane
San Francisco, California 94102

Dear Consumer:

We are pleased to provide this transcript of the credit information maintained by Credit Data Corporation under the name and address(es) you have submitted to us.

If you disagree with any of the information shown below, we want to know. Please use the following procedure:

PRINT the reason you disagree with the item(s) in the "CONSUMER COMMENTS" column next to the item. Be sure to sign on the reverse side and return this top copy to Credit Data Corporation in the enclosed envelope provided for your convenience. If additional space is required, feel free to use the "ADDITIONAL COMMENTS" area on the reverse side of this form.

IDENTIFICATION YOU SUPPLIED, ABBREVI-ATED FOR THE COMPUTER TO FIND YOUR FILE: SMITH, MARY, FOSTER LANE 12345, S-000000000

CONSUMER COMMENTS (IF ANY)

ATTN FILE VARIATION: SS# IS 000000000/OTHER FILE IDENT: MID INIT IS C

SOCIAL SECURITY NUMBER REPORTED AS 000000000

EMPLOYMENT: SELF—REPORTED IN 8-79

NAME AND ADDRESS: Mary C. Smith/ Foster Lane 20020

(POS:AUTOMATED) CURRENT ACCOUNT RE-PORTED IN 7/79 BY CITIBANK/J. MAGNIN—

CHARGE ACCT—CREDIT LIMIT OR HIGHEST
AMOUNT $800—REVOLVING CHARGE—ACCT
OPENED IN 11/70—ACCT #10000—AS OF 7/1/79
THE ACCOUNT BALANCE WAS $90—AC-
COUNT ASSOCIATION -1- INDIVIDUAL

(POS:AUTOMATED) CURRENT ACCOUNT RE-
PORTED IN 7/77 BY SPIEGELS—CHARGE
ACCT—CREDIT LIMIT OR HIGHEST AMOUNT
$350—REVOLVING CHARGE—ACCT OPENED
IN 7/72—ACCT #20000—AS OF 8/30/79 THE AC-
COUNT BALANCE WAS $0.

(POS:AUTOMATED) CLOSED ACCOUNT/PAID
SATISFACTORY REPORTED IN 1/79 BY UNITED
CALIFORNIA BANK—CHECKING ACCOUNT
CREDIT OR LINE OF CREDIT—CREDIT LIMIT
$500—REVOLVING TERMS—ACCT OPENED
IN 1/74—ACCT #30000 ACCOUNT ASSOCIA-
TION -1- INDIVIDUAL.

(POS:AUTOMATED) CURRENT ACCOUNT RE-
PORTED IN 6/79 BY CALIF CANADIAN BANK—
AUTO CONTRACT—ORIGINAL AMOUNT
$25,000—FOR 60 MONTHS—ACCT OPENED IN
9/78—ACCT #40000—AS OF 6/30/79 THE AC-
COUNT BALANCE WAS $21,200—ACCOUNT AS-
SOCIATION -1- INDIVIDUAL.

(POS:AUTOMATED) CURRENT ACCOUNT RE-
PORTED IN 9/79 BY BULLOCKS—CHARGE
ACCT—CREDIT LIMIT OR HIGHEST AMOUNT
$500—REVOLVING CHARGE—ACCT OPENED
IN 11/72 ACCT #50000—AS OF 9/11/79 THE AC-
COUNT BALANCE WAS $59—ACCOUNT ASSO-
CIATION -1- INDIVIDUAL.

This information is in error; I do not have an account with this store.

(NON:MANUAL) INQUIRY REPORTED IN 12/78
BY BLOOMINGDALE BROTHERS

(NON:AUTOMATED) INQUIRY BY CALIF CA-
NADIAN BANK IN 7/79—CHECKING ACCT
CREDIT OR LINE OF CREDIT

(NON:AUTOMATED) INQUIRY BY STANDARD
OIL IN 11/76—CREDIT CARD—REVOLVING
TERM

worth accounting sheet that lists assets on one side and debits on the other. (See Appendix I.)

I start with checking accounts. One of the reasons for going through the process step by step is to expose the soft spots, the deficiencies, in your current situation, and one place where I find a surprising amount of poorly used dollars is in the checking account statement. More than once, I've encountered new clients who have had more than $100,000 in their checking accounts. Granted, that's a problem most of us would like to have, but there is no sense in throwing away cash, which is exactly what happens when money sits for any length of time in a checking account. Even a simple passbook account, with 5½ percent interest, helps to offset the effects of erosion by inflation. The amounts involved don't have to be in six figures to be important.

I strongly recommend keeping just enough money in a checking account to cover the current month's expenses. Commonly, though, people who have received a large check will deposit it in a checking account until they have time to think about what they want to do with it. That short while has a way of turning into a long stretch of time, and that large sum has a way of dribbling out in small chunks until there's not much left. Banks love to see people like that coming through the door.

The next item on the checklist is the savings account. Ideally, it's good to have on deposit an amount equal to three to six months' after-tax earnings. The money isn't used for investing; it's simply an emergency fund. This need not be a passbook account. It can consist of an account at a credit union, money market funds—anything that will draw a reasonable amount of interest yet is accessible at a day's notice.

Then there is money that you are lending to an institution, which in turn lends it out to someone else at a higher rate. Certificates of deposit—with which you receive an interest rate that is higher than the passbook rate, in return for promising to leave that money on deposit for a certain period of time—are one example. Government bonds and corporate and municipal bonds all fall into the same category. I ask clients and students the cash value of their life insurance policies. Usually the question doesn't click until I ask them how much money they can borrow on their policies. Most life insurance policies are simply another form of loaned dollars, for you are lending money to the insurance company with the understanding that the money eventually will be returned to you at a set rate of interest.

"Working dollars" is another item on the balance sheet. This includes stocks and mutual funds and real estate. Though no stock is worth more than what it can be sold for on any given day, it's still important to know when each stock was purchased and the original cost. These have some important tax implications; thus, they are necessary in accurately figuring net worth.

Real estate is included in this category of working dollars, and that brings up what is usually the biggest item on a balance sheet: the family home, commonly the most promising source of money when you decide to start doing things with the net worth that you have accumulated.

It wasn't always that way. Few of us anticipated ten or twenty years ago that the home we bought would actually be a valuable investment. We expected that we would buy a house as a necessity, that it would have a fairly fixed value over the years, and that the value of the house would remain fairly constant. Of course, that's no longer the case. What was a $30,000 house ten years ago may be a $90,000 house today. The house that $30,000 bought ten years ago is hardly the same house that $30,000 will buy today, if, indeed, you can even find a $30,000 house anymore.

Any other kind of real estate ought to be listed on the net worth balance sheet—a vacation home, raw land, even a condominium that you might own on a time-sharing basis. As with every other item on this list, you'll need to know the market value of the property. In the case of real estate, it's important not to take the tax assessor's word too seriously. We all complain about taxes, but most of our homes could be sold for a good deal more than the assessed value. There are several different ways of getting good appraisals. One of those is to pay for one from a professional appraiser. Also, a competent real estate brokerage firm is usually more than happy to send out representatives to take a good look at your home if they know that you may be ready to sell the property. That opinion is usually quite accurate, as long as you discount the figure that you're given by a few thousand dollars. Naturally, the brokerage house is anxious to get a listing and the agent will most likely give you a figure so high that you can't afford not to sell. With that automatic deduction, though, the quote from a good real estate agent is usually quite accurate.

Finally, one of the simplest ways of getting a good idea of the market value of your own home is to see what similar houses in your own neighborhood have brought on the market lately. The value of your own home is probably quite close.

The next category on the checklist is limited partnerships. It's difficult to determine the value of these. Usually I simply use the original dollar investment. This holds true for most partnerships, except for real estate. Often the general partner can give an updated evaluation of her respective property.

The next items on the list are collectibles. These include art, diamonds, collections of stamps, coins, jewelry—anything of intrinsic value. It's necessary to have a good appraisal of these things at least once a year. Most appraisers will be able to revise an earlier appraisal of any items they have previously done for you at a minimal cost. Your previous appraisal will have a description of the item as well as a photograph. Simply present that, and an update will be made, reflecting the current (usually increased) value of the item.

Other items of value are personal property, which most people tend to undervalue. Consider, though, the expense of replacing your furniture, car, and so on, and you'll discover that your personal property is probably worth much more than you would expect.

The total of the numbers in all these categories constitutes your total assets. On the debit side are any mortgages, installment payments, second deeds of trusts, home improvement or other loans, and payments to Mastercharge, Macy's, VISA, and the like. Then you subtract your total liabilities from your total assets. The assets are supposed to be greater than the liabilities. If they're not, you have a problem. But that's the whole purpose of doing a balance sheet like this, pointing out the problems so that something can be done about them.

Sometimes a whole change in lifestyle is necessary. One of my clients is a single woman in her twenties making over $20,000 a year. When she came to me, she was discouraged because she couldn't save any money on a good salary and because so much of her money was going out in taxes. I had her break down her expenses in detail. I discovered that she was commuting nearly 100 miles to work each day, living in an expensive apartment, and eating in restaurants four or five times a week because it was just too much of a chore to fix dinner after she'd spent a day at work and then wasted an hour or more behind the wheel. I urged her to move closer to work; she did and saved not only bridge tolls, gas, money, and wear on her automobile but also more than two hours of driving every day, more than ten hours a week. She found a place to live that was less expensive than the one she had left. She put herself on a budget, began eating most of her meals at home, and saved the cost of restaurant food. After a few months she had done so well that I was able to recommend her for a $5,000 bank loan because she had demonstrated the ability to discipline herself and save. With the money she was able to buy into a real estate limited partnership that gave her considerable tax savings and also returned a good yield on her investment. All this was possible because she made the effort to sit down and fill in all the blanks on that net worth balance sheet and saw in plain numbers how dismal her financial situation was.

The final figure is just a starting point, however. There are intangibles that must be taken into account as well. One of these is the sources of your income, the amount of it, and its reliability. Your net worth may be negligible, but if you have good, reliable earning potential, then you've got a lot going for you. Another factor is your willingness and ability to take risks. Often your financial objective and your risk-taking abilities go hand in hand. Some of my clients have told me that they'd like to take a $10,000 investment and triple it within a year. But, they're quick to add, they don't want to take the chance of losing it. That sort of thing just doesn't happen.

Another important factor in assessing yourself as an investor is your borrowing power. You will want to have capital available for investment, but if your credit record and your income are good, the chances are excellent that you'll be able to find a bank to lend you the money that you need to begin investing and reducing your taxes.

The final figure on the balance sheet can be misleading, too, if the holdings aren't diversified or if you're unwilling to take the dollars out and put them to work. Net worth doesn't mean as much if it is tied up in a home that you don't wish to refinance, in art or jewelry that you want to retain, in a limited partnership to which you're committed and which you cannot liquidate, or even in a stock that you think you can't afford to sell. An investor with moderate liquid assets, and a modest net worth, but with a willingness to commit her dollars, has greater potential as an investor than another with a higher net worth but no liquid assets and no willingness to convert her latent dollars into investment capital.

Many people have negligible liquid assets and a net worth of zero or less. Even so, there is still hope for most of these people. The vehicle that they need to begin their financial restructuring has been in their hands all along, though it has unfortunately slipped through their fingers before they had a chance to hold it. It rests, conveniently enough, in the Internal Revenue Service's Form 1040.

3

HOW TO MINIMIZE TAXES

AT this point, a short trip to your files is in order. The time
has come to confront your adversary face to face. Find a copy
of your latest tax return and a recent accounting stub from
one of the paychecks that probably provides the bulk—if not
the entirety—of your income. On the tax return, note the
figure that represents the total income tax you paid last year.
On the paycheck stub, look for the amount of money that is
withheld from your salary, by federal law, every pay period.

Those numbers are your enemies in your efforts to achieve
a solid financial footing. They are your obstacles to almost any
financial strategy, whatever your ultimate objective.

Probably those figures seem appallingly high to you. No
mistake there; most people could pay far less income tax than
they do and still remain in the good graces of the Internal
Revenue Service. Much of your early effort in executing a
financial strategy will be directed to whittling down, by legal
means, the size of those numbers. It is an effort that will be
constant for as long as you seriously pursue your goal of
financial success. Don't let the magnitude of those numbers
discourage you, for they represent not only a challenge, but
also the source of much of the capital with which you will
become a serious investor.

That is the thrust of the chapter—to acquaint you more
fully with taxes and to show you how you can, by legal
methods, stop the flow of many of your tax dollars into that
bottomless hole from which they can never be retrieved and
divert that money into the creative investments that are a

major part of any sound financial plan. Chances are that much of the money that you now automatically pay in income taxes can be used to turn you into a creative investor, without changing your lifestyle or standard of living one bit.

I stress that all this is perfectly legal. The methods I advocate are sanctioned and even encouraged by the laws under which the federal government taxes our incomes.

There may be some who feel a moral compulsion to pay taxes. That is an impulse that I don't share. I feel that the money that I've managed to divert from the Internal Revenue Service into legitimate investments has helped me and my family far more than it would have otherwise. Nor have I ever been reticent to reclaim money by any means that the IRS allows. The government, after all, is never bashful about passing laws to claim all that it might require. I dislike the term "loophole" for the methods that I will advocate in the next few pages. The word has a slightly disreputable connotation. It implies an oversight on the part of the government that allows a few canny operators to escape their obligations, like kids sneaking into a movie theater through a backdoor.

The truth is that these methods are available to everyone who pays taxes. They are practiced by our most respected citizens. They are not accidents; they exist for a purpose, with the full knowledge and countenance of the IRS. And they exist, for the most part, because our lawmakers have decided that they will stimulate our national economy.

For my part, then, I don't try to avoid unnecessary taxes just for the sake of my own financial status (though that's certainly a compelling reason). I feel I'm doing it for the benefit of my family and for the very necessary growth of the economy. I truly feel that avoiding unnecessary taxes is something of a duty, for if the IRS suddenly ended all the means by which people avoid income taxes, it would end a most important source of investment capital for the new business ventures that supply jobs and keep the national economy vital.

And if that argument alone isn't compelling enough, if you still need to be convinced of the necessity of reducing the adjusted gross income on which your taxes are based, consider the graduated tax schedule used by the IRS and how it penalizes taxpayers in direct proportion to increases in their incomes.

Study the shortened version of the IRS tax tables that is provided here. Each step upward in adjusted gross income represents an increase in the tax bracket about which we all have heard so much. Most people, however, don't truly understand the concept.

Take the phrase "49 percent bracket." That doesn't mean that half the total income of a person in that bracket is going out in taxes. It does mean, however, that all the income *beyond* that level is taxed at the 49 percent rate—until the next bracket is reached, that is, when the rate goes up even more.

For a single taxpayer, the 49 percent level is $34,100. (See tables.) A person with an adjusted gross income of exactly $34,100 will pay exactly $9,766 in federal income taxes. Any income beyond that level is taxed at 49 percent. So an additional $1,000, say, tacked onto that adjusted gross income of $34,100 will be taxed for $490, or 49 percent. That rate holds until the adjusted gross income reaches $41,500. Any income above that amount is taxed at 55 percent.

For married taxpayers filing jointly, the 49 percent bracket is reached at an adjusted gross income of $45,800. Any income beyond that is taxed at 49 percent, unless it exceeds the next increment, $60,000. This means that married couples with a joint income of $60,000 pay nearly $8,000 more in taxes than married couples with a gross income of $45,000. Their taxes will nearly double while their income rises just $15,000, and the effect is even more painful higher up on the scale.

The tax brackets are obviously no encouragement to increasing your income. I don't like to see any of my clients in a 49 percent bracket. Even those who reduce their tax

Revised Individual Tax Rate Schedule

(As Established by the 1978 Tax Reform Act)

SCHEDULE I: Single Taxpayers Who Do Not Qualify for Rates
in Schedules II or III

If the Amount of Taxable Income Is		The Tax Is		
Over—	But Not Over—			Of Excess Over—
$ 2,300 — $ 3,400		$ 0	plus 14%	— $ 2,300
$ 3,400 — $ 4,400		$ 154	plus 16%	— $ 3,400
$ 4,400 — $ 6,500		$ 314	plus 18%	— $ 4,400
$ 6,500 — $ 8,500		$ 692	plus 19%	— $ 6,500
$ 8,500 — $ 10,800		$ 1,072	plus 21%	— $ 8,500
$ 10,800 — $ 12,900		$ 1,555	plus 24%	— $ 10,800
$ 12,900 — $ 15,000		$ 2,059	plus 26%	— $ 12,900
$ 15,000 — $ 18,200		$ 2,605	plus 30%	— $ 15,000
$ 18,200 — $ 23,500		$ 3,565	plus 34%	— $ 18,200
$ 23,500 — $ 28,800		$ 5,367	plus 39%	— $ 23,500
$ 28,800 — $ 34,100		$ 7,434	plus 44%	— $ 28,800
$ 34,100 — $ 41,500		$ 9,766	plus 49%	— $ 34,100
$ 41,500 — $ 55,300		$ 13,392	plus 55%	— $ 41,500
$ 55,300 — $ 81,000		$ 20,982	plus 63%	— $ 55,300
$ 81,800 — $ 108,300		$ 37,677	plus 68%	— $ 81,800
$ 108,300		$ 55,697	plus 70%	— $ 108,300

SCHEDULE II: Married Taxpayers Filing Joint Returns, and Certain Widows and Widowers
Schedules II or III

If the Amount of Taxable Income Is		The Tax Is		
Over—	But Not Over—			Of Excess Over—
$ 3,400 — $ 5,500		$ 0	plus 14% —	$ 3,400
$ 5,500 — $ 7,600		$ 294	plus 16% —	$ 5,500
$ 7,600 — $ 11,900		$ 630	plus 18% —	$ 7,600
$ 11,900 — $ 16,000		$ 1,404	plus 21% —	$ 11,900
$ 16,000 — $ 20,200		$ 2,265	plus 24% —	$ 16,000
$ 20,200 — $ 24,600		$ 3,273	plus 28% —	$ 20,200
$ 24,600 — $ 29,900		$ 4,505	plus 32% —	$ 24,600
$ 29,900 — $ 35,200		$ 6,201	plus 37% —	$ 29,900
$ 35,200 — $ 45,800		$ 8,162	plus 43% —	$ 35,200
$ 45,800 — $ 60,000		$ 12,720	plus 49% —	$ 45,800
$ 60,000 — $ 85,600		$ 19,678	plus 54% —	$ 60,000
$ 85,600 — $ 109,400		$ 33,502	plus 59% —	$ 85,600
$ 109,400 — $ 162,400		$ 47,544	plus 64% —	$ 109,400
$ 162,400 — $ 215,400		$ 81,464	plus 68% —	$ 162,400
$ 215,400		$ 117,504	plus 70% —	$ 215,400

liabilities to the 35 percent bracket may still pay state taxes that bring them back up to a total tax commitment near the 50 percent bracket. (Some states do not collect taxes. More common, however, is the practice in the state of California, for example, where an adjusted gross income of $32,620 for a married couple filing jointly and $16,310 for an individual is taxed at 11 percent. This rate is one of the highest in the nation.) By now, though, you won't be surprised to hear that I don't advocate keeping your income deliberately low so that you won't be taxed too much.

My solution is to look for deductions, shelters, and deferrals that will allow you to increase your money without increasing the taxes you pay. Investments cost money. That doesn't necessarily mean that you'll have to stop buying steak, that you can't afford the new car you've been hoping to buy. Ideally, the money for your investments will come from the dollars you save by reducing your tax burden.

Best of all, you don't have to wait for a whopping refund check in the spring to begin enjoying the benefits. My clients rarely receive refunds of more than a couple of hundred dollars. A refund check, after all, is simply the IRS's way of giving back to you what was already yours. By using the W-4 form that stipulates the amount of taxes withheld from their regular paycheck, my clients ensure that the IRS never gets more than that to which it is legally entitled.

If you have ever held a regular job, you've almost surely seen a W-4. Probably it was given to you in your company's accounting office. You were asked whether you were married and the number of dependents you would claim, and then you were told to sign. At that point, you had given the Internal Revenue Service license to withhold a predetermined amount from your paycheck. It may have amounted to more than you needed to be paying, and refund checks don't include interest.

So you need to become far more familiar with the W-4, and the best way I can help you do that and show you the overall benefits of a tax and investment plan is by citing a couple of case histories of clients of mine. Very likely, your situation is somewhat similar to one of these two.

In the previous chapter I mentioned the young professional woman who had disciplined herself in order to improve her financial situation. She is typical of one type of client, a young woman with a salary between $15,000 and $25,000 who lives from paycheck to paycheck, never getting the full benefits of a good salary.

This woman had an annual income of $22,000, out of which she paid over $4,500 in federal and state taxes. She had $500 in a savings account, received no alimony although she was divorced, owned no stock or real estate, and had no investments. I've told how she managed to save money, qualify for a loan, and invest in a real estate partnership. But I haven't mentioned how that investment affected her taxes.

Using the $5,000 she had borrowed, she invested with thirty partners in an apartment house in a northern California town. Her tax benefits included the tax-deductible interest on her personal loan ($600 the first year) and the overall benefits of the partnership ($1,400, which is reflected on line 18 of IRS Form 1040, relating to partnerships, pensions, etc., thereby reducing her overall income).

She began keeping track of her itemized deductions, including business-related expenses for which she was not reimbursed, and at the end of the year she found that she had exceeded the $2,300 minimum that is the standard for nonitemized returns. She had made contributions to charitable agencies that she had never before itemized; she had purchased a car that she used in her business, and on which there was a large sales tax and registration fee. She had paid interest on her auto loan and $1,400 in state taxes. Her total of itemized deductions was over $5,500—not at all out of line for a woman with her job as a salesperson and her income.

Her taxable income, which had been $22,000, was reduced to $16,500. By adjusting the number of exemptions listed on her W-4 form, she was able to take immediate advantage of her deductions. A glance at the W-4 form and tables in the accompanying figure shows exactly how she accomplished this.

First she entered her estimated annual deduction of $5,500 on line E1 of the "Worksheet to Figure Your Withholding Allowances to be Entered on line 1 of Form W-4"; then she used the table provided in section E2 to determine the number of excess deductions to which that $5,500 entitled her. The method is less complicated than it may seem. Since she was a single employee with only one job and an annual salary of $22,000, she entered $2,800 on line 2 and subtracted that from $5,500, leaving her with $2,700 (line E3). That number was divided by $1,000 to produce the number of excess deductions she could claim. Her number was 2.7, and since instructions permit rounding up to the next whole number, she claimed three excess deductions on line E. According to the general instructions (which are not shown here but appear on the reverse side of the W-4 form in your employer's office), you may also claim one special withholding allowance if you are single and have one job or if you are married and have one job and your spouse does not work. Since the woman in this example met the first set of conditions, she entered 1 on line B, which gave her a total of five exemptions (line F), including the personal exemption (line A) to which she was automatically entitled. With those five exemptions, she increased her weekly pay check and decreased withholding enough to more than cover the monthly loan payment on her original $5,000. She was even able to set aside more money to invest at a later date.

If she had not adjusted her exemptions, she would have received a large refund when she filed her income taxes the following year. The disadvantage of that becomes immediately apparent when you consider that the IRS pays no interest at all on refunds. Rather than letting the government use your money interest-free, you can adjust your W-4 form and start putting the money to work in investments and interest-bearing savings plans.

Form W-4 (Rev. 10-79)

Tax Credit Table for Figuring Your Withholding Allowances—See Example Below

Allowances ▶	0	1		2		3		4		5		6	
Estimated salaries and wages from all sources:	Under	At least	But less than	At least	But less than	At least	But less than	At least	But less than	At least	But less than	At least	But less than

Part I Single Employees

No additional allowances

Salary	0	1 At least	1 But less than	2 At least	2 But less than	3 At least	3 But less than	4 At least	4 But less than
Under $5,000		250	500	500	700	700	900	900 or more	
5,000–15,000		350	700	700	1,000	1,000 or more			
15,001–25,000		550	950	950 or more					
25,001–35,000									

Part II Head of Household Employees

No additional allowances

Salary	0	1 At least	1 But less than	2 At least	2 But less than	3 At least	3 But less than	4 At least	4 But less than
Under $5,000		150	400	400	650	650	900	900 or more	
5,000–20,000		1	300	300	650	650	1,000	1,000 or more	
20,001–35,000		450	850	850 or more					
35,001–45,000									

Part III Married Employees (When Spouse is Not Employed)

No additional allowances

Salary	0	1 At least	1 But less than	2 At least	2 But less than	3 At least	3 But less than	4 At least	4 But less than	5 At least	5 But less than	6 At least	6 But less than
Under $8,000		200	350	350	500	500	700	700	800	800	950	950 or more	
8,000–15,000		250	500	500	700	700	950	950 or more					
15,001–25,000		300	650	650	950	950 or more							
25,001–35,000		650	1,050	1,050 or more									
35,001–45,000													

Part IV Married Employees (When Both Spouses are Employed)

No additional allowances

Salary	0	1 At least	1 But less than	2 At least	2 But less than	3 At least	3 But less than
Under $8,000		250	400	400	450	450 or more	
8,000–15,000		550	800	800	950	950 or more	
15,001–25,000							

Example: A taxpayer who expects to file a Federal income tax return as a single person estimates annual wages of $12,000 and tax credits of $650. The taxpayer uses Part I for single employees. The $12,000 falls in the wage bracket of $5,000 to $15,000 in the left column. Reading in the shaded area to the right, $650 falls within the estimated tax credits bracket of At least 500 But less than 700. Looking to the top of the column, the taxpayer finds that 2 allowances are permitted. The taxpayer enters "2" on line D of the Worksheet below.

Worksheet to Figure Your Withholding Allowances to be Entered on Line 1 of Form W-4
(Letters on this worksheet are keyed to the letters in the line-by-line instructions on page 1)

A Personal allowances . . . . ▲ **A** | 1

B Special withholding allowance (not to exceed 1 allowance—see instructions on page 1) . ▲ **B** | 1

C Allowances for dependents . . . . ▲ **C** | 0

D Allowances for estimated tax credits (from Tax Credit Table for Figuring Your Withholding Allowances, above):
  1 Find your filing status under Part I, II, III, or IV of the table.
  2 Under your filing status, find your estimated salaries and wages in the left column.
  3 Read the shaded amounts across to the right until you get to the amount of your estimated tax credits.
  4 At the top of that column is the number of allowances you may take for your estimated tax credits. Enter the number of allowances . . . . . . ▲ **D** | 0

E Allowances for estimated itemized deductions and alimony:
  1 Enter the amount of your estimated itemized deductions, including alimony payments, for the year . . . . ▲ **1** | $5500
  2 Find your total estimated salaries and wages amount in the left column of the table below. Read across to the right and enter the amount from the column that applies to you. Enter that amount here (if claiming only alimony payments on line E1, enter "0" on line E2). . . . ▲ **2** | *$ 2800

Estimated salaries and wages from all sources:	Single Employees (only one job)	Married Employees (one spouse working and one job only)	Employees with more than one job or Married Employees with both spouses working
Under $10,000	$2,800	$3,900	$4,000
*10,000–30,000	2,800	3,900	5,800
30,001–40,000	3,500	3,900	8,000
Over $40,000	15% of estimated salaries and wages	13% of estimated salaries and wages	23% of estimated salaries and wages

  3 Subtract line E2 from line E1. . . . . **3** | $ 2700
  4 Divide the amount on line E3 by $1,000 (round-off fractions to the nearest whole number). Enter here . ▲ **E** | 2.7 = 3

F Total (add lines A through E). Enter total here and on line 1 of Form W-4 . ▲ **F** | 5

In summary, then: where before this young woman had automatically paid out a considerable portion of her weekly check in income taxes, she now was part owner of a lucrative investment, she was saving money in a passbook account, and she had not disturbed her personal budget to do it. Her tax savings more than covered the cost.

I also like to cite the more complex example of a young couple who came to me not long ago, disturbed because they seemed to be treading water with a combined income of $50,000 a year. They were a classic example of a type I encounter too frequently. They owned a home in which they had considerable equity, they enjoyed eating out and entertaining, and they took a vacation once a year. They owned life insurance but had no real savings, few stocks, no true investments. They were in their mid-thirties. They paid less than $300 a month on a 7.5 percent mortgage with unpaid principal of $23,000, a situation not at all unusual in the San Francisco area, where I work and live. There, as in many other areas, increases in real estate values over the last decade have turned the family home into an important investment, quite often the single most important source of investment dollars.

I urged them to put those dollars to work by refinancing the house. This would have meant taking out a mortgage of $75,000 at 10 percent with which to pay off the existing loan. The remainder would be used for investment and emergency savings.

The woman was nervous about this plan. Payments on the new mortgage would be nearly $800 a month, including taxes, and she couldn't see how they would be able to pay that when they had been struggling already. I convinced her by showing her that in federal taxes alone, she and her husband were paying over $13,000 every year. (They barely exceeded the standard deduction level for their income level.) The money to pay that mortgage, I told her, would come out of that $13,000.

This was my plan:

• They refinanced the house, which gave them an extra $52,000 after the original mortgage had been paid off. The loan origination fee for this transaction was 1½ points— 1.5 percent of the amount of the loan—or $1,125. (They paid this fee with a separate check, which is a tactic that I'll go into later).

• Five thousand of the $52,000 went into a bank savings account for the emergency fund that I always recommend. At that time, passbooks and money market funds paid about the same interest rates. A savings and loan paid .25 percent more than the bank but offered fewer services. Therefore, we chose the bank to preserve these liquid funds.

• The largest investment was $20,000, divided equally into two real estate limited partnerships. The benefits of these enterprises—taxes, depreciation, management fees—provided a write-off of about 25 percent of the original investment, or $5,000.

• Another $5,000 went into a combined developmental-exploratory oil and gas program. Write-offs for these programs vary with the risk. This one, with fairly certain expectations of producing crude oil and natural gas, carried a first-year write-off of 80 percent, or $4,000.

• Another $5,000 was invested in a research and development program for a product that was still two years away from the marketplace. IRS rules permitted a 200 percent write-off since the partnership had taken out a bank loan that each of the partners was liable for. Because of this unusual structure, the $5,000 put into this program produced a $10,000 write-off. (This is an extremely high-risk investment.)

• The interest on the new mortgage was approximately $7,500 a year, all tax deductible.

• Real estate taxes were $1,000 a year, also tax deductible.

• My firm's counseling fees for the year were $1,000. Commissions are not tax deductible, but investment advice is.

• At my urging, both these clients took a closer look at some of the deductions they had been missing. His contributions, sales taxes, nonreimbursed business expenses, and others totaled $5,000.

• The money that remained—more than $20,000—was set aside for next year. Tax planning is more than a one-year enterprise. Most people need three years to get things turned in a favorable direction. Your tax bill will inevitably return to its former overblown proportions without proper planning each year. In this particular case, the couple would not be getting the benefits of the exotic research project the following year. The oil and gas benefits would be reduced, and there would be no repeat of the loan origination fee.

• Using the W-4 tables, the couple came up with $22,825 in excess deductions. They adjusted their W-4 forms. They claimed 23 total exemptions; he assumed 13, and she took 10. Their tax liability was reduced to $3,000, but instead of awaiting a $10,000 refund at the end of the year, they reduced their withholding by $5,900. His withholding went from $393 a month to $120. Hers was reduced from $393 to $170. The combined difference was $496. They were paying $5,200 a year extra for the mortgage, which was more than offset by their annual savings of $10,000. What was left over could be used for extra savings, more investments, or the luxury of an expensive trip or new furniture. Moreover, the couple now had stakes in several potentially lucrative investments. At the end of the first year they would assess their investments and plan their deductions for the following year without the pressure of the April 15 deadline. That would give them the very necessary chance to evaluate potential investments for their overall benefit, not simply for tax consequences. (I've found that, especially in gas and oil, the most attractive investments are offered in the first half of the year. The least viable seem to spring up in the last quarter, when investors are scrambling for almost any tax break.) The third year, the liquidation of their real estate holdings would give them the means to continue their investment program. They were on their way to achieving a solid financial footing, without having changed their lifestyle one iota.

It ought to be stressed again that neither they nor the young woman of the first example had once crossed into debatable legal areas in any of their tax dealings. It's simply not necessary that huge amounts be withheld from your paycheck if you have the proper deductions to back up a lesser figure. IRS instructions on the W-4 form are explicit: The taxpayer is urged not to overwithhold or underwithhold. The IRS doesn't really want to send you a massive refund check at the end of the year. The odds are that if you receive a check in excess of $200, the withholding sum was too great.

DEDUCTIONS

In each of these two examples, a close examination of expenditures showed that my clients were failing to claim all the deductions to which they were entitled. Women who are serious about a financial plan need to become familiar with what can be deducted, and how to substantiate these deductions.

Recordkeeping is vital. Receipts are one way to keep records, and a detailed and accurate journal or desk calendar helps to back up these receipts. Ideally, such a journal ought to record the miles driven for business purposes, with destinations and reasons for the trip, meals and incidental expenses that can be applied to business uses, the reason for that expense, the names of people involved (as in a business lunch), and the nature of the business discussed.

For women in the business of meeting clients or selling products, or those who need a car in the course of their work, the expense of an automobile can be partially or totally written off. I personally claim 90 percent of the expenses of operating my car. The IRS usually questions any figure over 90 percent, but I can back up my claim with records that show I drive to lectures, business conferences, meetings with clients, and trips to property in the area in which I've invested or in which I might be interested in investing.

• Donations of clothing usually can be claimed at 25 percent of fair market value.

• State tax is deductible. So is sales tax. Again, keep records. There is a minimum figure for your income level, but chances are that you'll exceed it any year when you buy a new car, or refurnish a home, or buy several large appliances.

• Car registration over $11 is deductible.

• Health insurance premiums can be deducted, up to $150.

• You probably know that medical and dental expenses are deductible, beyond a certain minimum that is calculated by your adjusted gross income. You might not be aware, however, that transportation to doctors' offices and hospitals is included in that category.

• Interest on loans can be an important deduction, and there is no limit on the amount of personal interest that can be deducted. Interest on home mortgages is generally the largest single item, but interest on car loans, credit cards, charges, and installment loans is equally valid.

There is a $10,000 limit on investment interest. Beyond that, each dollar of interest must be offset by a dollar of unearned income, such as dividends from stocks, interest payments on notes you may hold, or bond payments.

• Non-reimbursed business expenses can take many forms, and the key is accurate recordkeeping. This is especially important for salespeople; for whom it is one of the most frequently audited items. I keep separate business and personal credit cards, which simplifies the work. On the back of each receipt I write the date, the persons involved, the business discussed.

It's not necessary to have a formal lunch or dinner at a restaurant to qualify for this deduction. Dinners at home can be business-related too. Keep a guest list, a menu of the food served, and a grocery receipt. At today's prices, $10 per person is a reasonable expense. Naturally, you're allowed only to claim expenses for those who are actually involved in this business dinner.

You may find it helpful to your business to join various clubs or organizations. The dues are deductible. Pay by check and you've got a good receipt. (Most women will not be affected by a 1978 ruling that bans dues for duck clubs and hunting lodges as business expenses.)

Theater tickets and tickets to sporting events can be deductible. It's best to buy them in series, then keep track of where they're distributed and for what purpose.

• Uniforms are deductible. So is the cost of any other special clothing that may be required: special shoes or hats, lab coats, restaurant costumes—almost any clothing that you wouldn't wear anywhere else but on the job.

• Stock market losses can be deducted and carried forward up to $3,000 a year. Larger losses can be spread out over as many years as necessary to offset the sum.

• As I said earlier, investment advisory fees are deductible, but not commissions. (It doesn't take much time dealing with taxes to realize that the way you designate a deduction can make a great deal of difference.) Accounting expenses are deductible. So are legal fees in evaluating an investment contract, or attorney's fees in collecting a bad debt.

• If you own investment real estate that could be classified as vacation-rental property, the IRS will allow you to deduct the expense of a two-week visit to inspect the property every year. You can stay on the premises during those periods only. Any more will jeopardize that property's status as a true investment. This section of the tax code was tightened considerably by the Tax Act of 1976, and rightfully so. It had been much abused up to that point. Now you must make a real effort to keep the property rented, especially during the peak vacation periods.

• Alimony paid is tax deductible. That's of more than theoretical interest to women these days. (I have a woman friend, for example, who is paying $1,000 monthly alimony for five years.) If you're receiving support payments, it's far preferable to have them designated as child support. Alimony *received* is taxable; child support received is not. Conversely, while alimony *paid* is tax deductible, child support payments are not. Again, it's all in the name.

• The Investment Tax Credit is important to those who need to buy permanent equipment or supplies for a business. This can be an earth-loader for a construction company, a typewriter for an author, fruit trees for a farmer. They're important because the credit—10 percent of the cost of the item—is deducted from the tax that you pay each year, right off the bottom line. While you're at it, buy quality equipment that will last the seven-year replacement term that the IRS specifies. Then, in addition to the investment tax credit allowance, you'll be able to deduct the equipment's depreciation in value over the course of its useful life.

• One of the deductions of which the IRS has been wary recently is offices in the home. I've known individuals who had legitimate claims simply ignore the opportunity of deducting them because they felt the tax benefits did not outweigh the probability of an audit and the inconvenience of arguing the point with an IRS agent. Still, though the deduction has been abused in the past, there are allowable claims. For example, representatives of cosmetics and notions firms can deduct the cost of setting aside a specific room for files, desk and telephone, and storage of the product, as long as the office or storage area is not supplied by the company that is represented.

• Political contributions are tax credits: $100 for a single person, $200 for a married couple.

• There are child care credits for children under fifteen who must be tended during working hours. These fees can be paid to grandparents, which introduces a useful feature of the tax codes. The expenses of educating normal children are not deductible. No single individual need file a return, however, for a year in which he or she earns less than $3,300. If you should own a business, therefore, it's feasible to pay your children up to $3,300 (a deductible expense), and let that sum then pay for their education. This tactic is quite legal—provided, of course, that the children actually do work for the business.

• Support of any member of the family, including parents, grandparents, and in-laws, can be claimed if you are responsible for more than half the cost of their care.

• Many states have energy tax credits open to those who install alternative energy devices (such as solar water heaters) or insulation in their homes. In many cases, the state allowances are more generous than those permitted by the IRS.

• Educational expenses are deductible as long as the purpose of the classes is to help you perform your job better. Once more, the distinction is fine and nomenclature is the key. A bookkeeper can deduct the cost of courses that she takes to become a more skilled bookkeeper. She cannot deduct courses that help her to become a CPA, since those would not be complementary to her present position.

• If you have investments, it's necessary for you to keep current not only on financial matters, but also on current events that may affect the value of your investments. Therefore, financial periodicals like *Forbes, Fortune,* and *The Wall Street Journal* are deductible. So, too, are the daily newspapers. Even so-called women's magazines are now carrying regular features on money and investments and are therefore deductible. (And so is the price of this book.)

Many of us have interests and hobbies that we have considered turning into businesses. The IRS rule is that you must make a legitimate effort to turn a profit. But many businesses are not profitable in the first couple of years of operation. If you're sincere in turning your hobby from a leisure-time pursuit to a real business, then you should begin keeping records of expenses and capital investments.

I discovered that one of my clients gave canoe lessons during the summer. Usually he would make about $2,000, which he had neglected to list as income. I took a closer look at this little enterprise and discovered, among other things, that he had bought a special canoe and that he had bought a station wagon specifically to transport it. With the depreciation, the Investment Tax Credit, maintenance, and other expenses, he had more than offset his income from the lessons. By listing the $2,000 income (which he was legally required to do in any case), he was also entitled to list deductions that would actually lower his taxable income.

The point is that incidental, ordinary expenses often are incurred in the course of business and are, therefore, deductible. One of my clients works for a major electronic game company. Once a year he visits his parents in the Midwest, driving to see them. But on the way he stops at various arcades in different parts of the country and demonstrates some of the company's newest products. This helps him to understand what consumers are looking for in games. He can evaluate the product, which helps him do his job better. The company does not compensate him for these trips, though it acknowledges that they are helpful to business. So my client keeps a very detailed record of where he has been and what he has done at each stop. He then deducts that expense on the next tax return. It's true that he finally visits his family at the end of all these stopovers, but that is only an incidental product of the trip. Deductions don't have to be unpleasant or wearisome. They can be enjoyable and still productive.

If you're contemplating starting your own business, you'll need to understand short-term and long-term losses and gains.

Net operating losses occur when short-term losses outweigh short-term gains during any reporting period. (The distinction between long- and short-term is simple; any transaction with a life over one year and one day is long term. The profit from the sale of a piece of real estate is taxed as a short-term gain if the property was bought and sold within a one-year, one-day period. After that, it's regarded as long term.)

Short-term gains from the sale of stock or the operation of a business are added to ordinary income. Long-term gain, however, is taxed by a method that guarantees a tax rate of no more than 28 percent, until a new tax act changes it. (There is a strong drive to reduce the taxes on long-term gains even further, to a maximum of 20 percent, which may go into effect in 1981.)

Long-term losses offset only 50 percent of their value in ordinary income each year, up to the $3,000 maximum. Long-term losses of $5,000 in one year, for example, represent a deduction of $2,500 from ordinary income. A long-term loss of $7,000 in a single year means a deduction of just $3,000, the maximum. In other words, you would be allowed to use only $6,000 of that $7,000 amount to offset ordinary income. The remaining $1,000 could be carried over to the next tax year, when it can be used to offset $500 in income.

• One of the advantages of the 1978 Tax Act was the $100,000 exclusion of tax from the sale of personal real property by those over fifty-five years of age. The stipulation is that the property has been maintained as a residence and that it has been occupied for three of the last five years. This can be an enormous tax relief. It could make sense now for a retired couple to move from the family home—worth, perhaps, in excess of $150,000—into a condominium costing $80,000. The $70,000 difference, which might ordinarily be subject to heavy taxes, would be clear profit, well under the $100,000 limit of the exclusion.

The tax break is so good that it may not be around for long. It is subject to repeal after officials have had a chance to evaluate its effect, and there is speculation that the monetary loss to the government will be so great that the exclusion will be either modified or totally ended. My recommendation is that you take advantage of it while you can, if you're eligible to do so.

• I noted earlier that the couple in my second example had paid for the cost of their loan—the 1½-point, $1,125 loan fee—with a separate check, rather than having the fee subtracted from the refinanced money they received or added onto the new loan, i.e., $76,125 instead of $75,000. The IRS has ruled that unless the fee is paid for separately, the cost is amortized over the life of the loan. That $1,125 is of negligible benefit when spread over 30 years.

RETIREMENT PROGRAMS

If you are self-employed or if you are employed by a company that does not cover you by a pension or profit-sharing program, you are entitled to begin such a program for yourself. This is called an Individual Retirement Account, (IRA). There are numerous advantages to an IRA, but the major one is the tax benefit. Contributions to an IRA account are fully deductible from your Federal income tax return. The income and profits earned while you maintain an IRA accumulate free of any tax consequence until money is withdrawn at a later date.

As of today, the maximum amount that you may contribute to any IRA account is up to 15 percent of your earnings, not to exceed $1,500, in any taxable year. You do not have to make contributions every year, and contributions can be paid any time during the year or up until the time you actually file your tax return, i.e., April 15. If you have been granted an extension until June 15, you have until that date to make your contributions for the preceding year.

If you are married and you and your spouse both work, you may each be able to establish an IRA if neither of you is covered under a pension plan or profit-sharing act for that year. If only one partner in a marriage is working and that person is not covered by a pension or profit-sharing plan, it is possible to set up a spousal IRA. This allows the working individual to contribute up to 15 percent of his or her earnings, not to exceed $1,500, plus an additional $250, or a maximum of $1,750. In a spousal IRA, the total amount of money contributed must be divided equally between the couple so that each has his or her own IRA.

If you are leaving one place of work and receive a distribution from a tax-qualified plan from your previous employer, you may, within sixty days, place it in what is called a Roll Over. The $1,500 limitation does not apply in this situation. This allows you to place these funds into another tax-qualified program without any tax consequences.

When you elect to make withdrawals from your IRA, that money will be treated as ordinary income and will be taxed at your current tax rate. If you withdraw funds before the age of fifty-nine-and-a-half, there will be, except if you die or are disabled, a penalty of 10 percent. Also, if you fail to make any withdrawals prior to the age of seventy, there will be a penalty.

If you put the money from your IRA account into one type of investment, i.e., a mutual fund or stocks or even the bank, you may change the investment and put it into another form of program the following year by establishing a new IRA. You are also allowed in one of every three years to take money from, for example, the bank and put it all into an IRA mutual fund without penalty, by rolling over from one type of IRA to another.

If you pay any taxes at all on the federal level and you are qualified to participate in an IRA program, you will not be paying the full $1,500, if that is what you are entitled to, of the cost. The $1,500 that you deposit will be deducted from your adjusted gross income and will thus reduce your taxes.

If you are self-employed—if, for example, you are a doctor, a lawyer, or an accountant or own a business of any kind that does not have a pension or profit-sharing plan—you could put together a Keogh plan. The Keogh is very similar to the IRA, but it allows you to put away up to 15 percent of $50,000, or a maximum of $7,500. The same stipulations as to withdrawals, contributions, tax advantages, and restrictions hold true for a Keogh account as for an IRA.

To receive additional information about IRA or Keogh plans, contact your local brokerage firm, a mutual fund, a bank, or the business section of your local newspaper. Many advertisements appear, especially toward the end of the year, offering other possibilities for ways to invest these special funds.

The chart below illustrates the benefit of placing $1,500 yearly over a thirty-year period in an IRA earning 7½ percent. The accumulated amount is shown for a spousal account in which $875, which represents half the $1,750, is allowed to earn interest at 8 percent for a total of thirty, thirty-five, and forty years. Quite often I find that most people think it is insignificant to place just a few hundred or a few thousand dollars aside every year, or whatever the case may be, but the following illustrations indicate that those dollars can substantially increase. With today's interest rates, which are significantly higher than 7½ percent, you should achieve even greater returns.

Years	Initial Contribution	Compound Interest @ 7½ percent
	$1,500 @ 7½ percent	
1	$ 1,500	$ 1,612
5	7,500	9,341
10	15,000	22,774
15	22,500	42,059
20	30,000	69,743
25	37,500	109,489
30	45,000	168,048
	$875 @ 8 percent	
30	$26,250	$ 99,122
35	30,625	150,776
40	35,000	226,673

TAX SHELTERS

To define the term: a tax shelter is any enterprise into which you invest money, expecting to realize a profit, and receive some tax benefits. Tax shelters can come in almost any form, set up around almost any undertaking. Some of the common ones involve oil and gas, movies, real estate, coal, leasing, cattle, and agriculture. They can come in the form of a joint venture—several people pooling their money to start a business, for example, and sharing the liability. They can be limited partnerships, in which the liability of the investors is only as great as the amount of their original investment, with the general partners being legally responsible for the operation of the enterprise. They can involve an individual's starting a business or buying an apartment house, assuming all the risk and taking all the profits that may accrue.

The variety of shelters is great, and each type of shelter has its own benefit. This is an area in which you will definitely need professional advice and guidance.

Oil and gas shelters have huge immediate benefits from the Investment Tax Credit with the purchase of new heavy machinery, intangible drilling costs, and the depletion allowance. The riskier the operation in terms of potential success, the greater the immediate benefit.

Pistachio trees have been a popular high-risk shelter, yielding the investor depreciation on the trees and an Investment Tax Credit from replacement of the trees.

Real estate is among the less spectacular shelters in terms of immediate tax benefits, but it also is a reliable investment and a fine hedge against inflation.

Be aware that any lucrative field attracts shady operators. Tax shelters are no exception. Quality investments, as I said earlier, are most prevalent at the beginning of the year. In the last quarter, poor offers are abundant, and too often they are snapped up by desperate taxpayers who, having put off planning too long, suddenly realize the extent of their tax liability and are willing to put their money into almost any shelter that will guarantee them momentary relief.

This is a mistake. There is no sense in avoiding taxes at the expense of your capital. Money lost in a bad deal is lost as surely as if it had been paid to the government. One of my favorite nonsense shelters was a beehive scheme into which a young doctor put several thousand dollars, producing a large and painful sting in his wallet. He now claims allergies to all tax shelters.

I'll discuss partnerships and joint ventures later, but for the moment it's important to state that tax benefits aren't sufficient reason to go into a shelter. You must examine the track record of the general partners and evaluate the feasibility of the project.

Remember that there are numerous other possible deductions, some of which may be applicable to you and your own tax situation. To be able to take advantage of them and to choose a shelter intelligently, you need to know your objectives and to anticipate changes that may be pending in your financial future. But tax laws are complex. New rulings and interpretations are made constantly, and only a trained financial counselor, accountant, or tax attorney can guide you through the ever-thickening maze.

Over the years in which I have counseled individuals, handling some very complicated cases and some small ones that most other advisers would not even consider taking on, I have come to the conclusion that all of us need some advice throughout our financial lives. An annual financial check-up, comparable to an annual physical, may save you from making a wrong financial decision and open up new possibilities that could be extremely beneficial. The expense is worthwhile and tax deductible. If you are one of the few who finds out that she is already doing everything right, you will have spent a few dollars and reconfirmed that all is well. (Any reputable adviser will quickly recognize that he or she has no help to give you and send you on your way with a minimal charge.) Chapter 11 will give you a number of tips on selecting professionals to work with.

4

WHAT TO DO ABOUT INFLATION

INFLATION is an economic phenomenon that has become a national news story and a political issue, and rightly so. Inflation has drastic effects on the nation's economy, on the ways we make money and spend it. Ultimately, when a high rate of inflation continues over several years, it affects our style of living. I urge you to understand inflation and all its ramifications before you begin to study any potential investment. The rate of inflation will be—or at least, *ought* to be—a factor in every financial decision you make. And the higher that rate, the more important a factor it is.

Inflation denotes a decrease in the purchasing power of a given amount of money. Goods and services become more valuable and more expensive; money is required in increasing amounts. Therefore, any given unit of money is less valuable. To use one basic example, we'll suppose that a year ago you could have bought ten of a certain item for $100. During the year, however, the price of that item has risen. The $100 that bought ten items a year earlier will now be enough to purchase only nine of that same item. The dollar buys one-tenth less than it did a year earlier, and the decline in purchasing power is measured as a 10 percent rate of inflation.

Or approach it from another angle. Assume that a dishwasher cost $500 a year ago. With a 10 percent rate of inflation, the same appliance now costs $550 ($500 plus 10 percent, or $50). Either way, the result is the same: The dollar buys less at any given time than it did in the past.

Money is worth less. And since inflation seems to be a permanent phenomenon, you can be reasonably sure that money will be worth less at any time in the future than it is now. The only question is how much less. The answer to that question will be the final determining factor in your decisions on many potential investments.

There are numerous theories about the causes of inflation. You don't need to know most of them. But economists do agree that one primary cause of higher prices is increased demand for goods and services, coupled with decreased supply of those things. That principle will help you to understand inflation and to project the rate at which it might grow in coming years. Basically, we have begun to shift from being a nation of producers to being one of consumers. Until that trend is reversed, inflation is likely to remain high. Look especially to government policies for a clue to the direction of the inflation rate in the future. The government, after all, is the most prodigious single consumer in this country. The bill is paid in two ways: by simply printing more money (thereby decreasing the value of money that already exists), and by borrowing. As we'll see soon, borrowers stand to profit most from a high inflation rate.

Inflation is harmful for a couple of reasons. When our dollar loses value, it also loses ground to the currency of other nations that produce more than they consume. West Germany and Japan are two prime examples. And often there is a natural, automatic slowdown in the economy as a reaction to rising inflation. This is a recession. Usually it tends to reduce the inflation rate, because it reduces the spending capability of consumers and hence reduces the demand for goods and services. But this is only at the price of high unemployment and financial disruption for many thousands of families.

There are winners and losers during periods of high inflation. The big winners are borrowers, using others' money to increase their own net worth and then repaying that money in dollars that have been reduced in value by inflation since the loan was made. The losers are the lenders. That doesn't mean large savings and loan companies, banks, or credit agencies. These institutions are not bound by usury laws and can raise their interest rates high enough to compensate for the declining value of the money they have lent out. But there are other lenders. You are a lender if you put money in savings accounts run by those banks and savings and loan companies. You're a lender if you hold a second trust deed or if you buy corporate or municipal bonds. Everyone with a fixed income (such as those depending on pensions, income from stocks and bonds, and Social Security payments) is a loser because that income stays fixed while prices rise and the value of money declines. Deed holders and those with a significant amount of money in savings accounts or time deposit accounts are hit just as hard because their income, the interest they receive from those accounts, is fixed either by federal banking law or by contract. Remember that you're not just putting your money in a safe place when you make a deposit in a savings account or time deposit plan. You're lending money to that bank or institution to use until you reclaim it. While you're being paid 5 or 6 percent, that money is being lent out at higher rates or put to even more lucrative uses.

The idea in inflationary times is first to retain the value of your assets despite the decline of the dollar and then to increase the rate of return until your wealth is actually growing faster than inflation can diminish its value.

A couple of examples will show just how important it is to be a borrower, not a lender, during inflationary times.

Assume that a woman has $5,000 in cash that she doesn't need for daily expenses. If she simply keeps it in a checking account, where it draws no interest, it will be worth $4,500 at the end of a year, presuming a 10 percent rate of inflation. If she lent the $5,000 sum at 10 percent interest, she would make $500 in interest by the end of the year. That interest, however, is subject to income tax. If the woman is in a 30 percent bracket, the tax on that $500 will be about $150, which reduces the figure to $350. Remember that the purchasing power of the dollar has declined 10 percent during the year, however. The original $5,000 plus the $350 interest actually will buy only what $4,815 would have bought the year before. (Subtract 10 percent of $5,350, or $535, to arrive at the adjusted value.) The situation is even more dismal if the woman decides to withdraw the $500 interest from the account at the end of the year and use that money for living expenses. That leaves her with an actual value of $4,315 at the end of one year after taxes and inflation have taken their toll.

Or presume, again, a 10 percent annual rate of inflation during a five-year period, and let's say that a woman is selling a house for $200,000. She has found a buyer at that price, but the buyer stipulates as part of the contract that the money be paid by $20,000 cash down payment, a $140,000 bank loan, and a $40,000 second deed of trust payable in five years, at 10 percent interest. Assume that the seller, who will be holding the $40,000 second deed of trust, is in a 30 percent tax bracket. The loan will yield $4,000 a year in interest, but taxes will be $1,200, leaving a net of $2,800. That amount is subject to 10 percent inflation, losing $280 of its value every year. So the true value of the interest payment is $2,520 each year ($2,800 minus $280). That total, over a five-year period, is $12,600. Now look at the declining purchasing power of the $40,000 principal. At the end of the first year, it loses 10 percent of its value, or $4,000, so that its true value after one year is $36,000. Subtract another 10 percent from that, and the value stands at $32,400 after two years. During the third and fourth years the value drops to $29,150 and $26,224. By the end of the fifth year, when the note finally becomes due, the real value of the $40,000 payment will be $23,622. The interest that has been paid during that time still doesn't make up the difference, once taxes and inflation have been taken into account.

Things would have been far different if the seller had demanded a full cash payout and put the proceeds in a tax-deferred annuity paying 10 percent. That way, she would at least have been able to keep abreast of inflation, with the interest compounding but not yet subject to income taxes.

She might have done even better if she had used the money to buy items that would increase in value faster than inflation increased. These are inflation "hedges" that traditionally hold their own against inflation's inroads. "Hedges against inflation" merely means items or investments that increase in value at a higher percentage annually than the rate for inflation. I'll discuss them in greater detail later in this chapter. At the moment, you should be aware that they are a part of any successful strategy to combat inflation's effect.

Inflation will make your financial decisions doubly difficult, for it closes off so many options that might otherwise be profitable. And it turns ordinarily safe investments into high-risk propositions.

Simple savings accounts, for example, are a hopeless means of trying to keep up with inflation. You're fighting a losing battle against 10 percent inflation if your savings account isn't even paying 6 percent. That's not to mention the additional effect of having to pay income tax on the interest. Certificates of deposit pay somewhat higher interest, but they carry penalties for early withdrawal, which eliminates any flexibility you might have with simple savings accounts. That means you're locked in to whatever rate is current when you make the deposit. If the interest rate should rise during that time, the value of your money will dwindle. The same is true of municipal and corporate bonds. Not only do their interest rates usually fail to match the rate of inflation, but their actual market value drops as the inflation rate rises. (In the section on bonds in Chapter Five, you will see exactly how that happens.)

History has shown that not only bonds but also securities have been poor performers during times of high inflation. One study shows that a typical diversified stock portfolio costing $10,000 in 1968 would have been worth about

$10,300 in 1979. With the effects of inflation during those intervening years, the actual value of the portfolio would have been about $5,500 in 1979 dollars.

But there are places that seem unaffected by rampant inflation. One of these is real estate. Well-located and productive farmland costing $10,000 in 1968 was worth about $29,000 eleven years later. Convert that $29,000 into 1968 dollars and the value is still $15,000, a nice profit. Because building costs have risen so sharply, the value of office buildings has increased markedly as well: The $10,000 investment of 1968 returned about $22,000 in 1979, or $11,500 in 1968 terms. Homes have shown a similar increase during that period. And real estate is especially attractive as a hedge because it often offers the chance to use others' money to make a profit, the most desirable situation to be in during inflationary periods.

A short example: Three years ago, a client of mine borrowed $5,000 from a bank as a personal loan, paying 12.25 percent interest. During the three-year period of the loan she paid $1,620 in interest. Since she was in a 36 percent tax bracket, the tax write-off on that interest was worth $583, so her actual expense for using the bank's money was just over $1,000.

She invested the money in a 48-unit apartment house, buying into a limited partnership. Because the partnership refurbished the building with landscaping, new carpets, and new paint, the new managers were able to rent the apartments for somewhat more than they had brought previously. This higher income made the property itself more valuable to investors, so when the partnership was liquidated after two years, the investors turned a 180 percent profit. That meant that, for each $5,000 invested, the limited partners received the original sum plus an additional $9,000. So for an actual cost of $1,037 (the original investment, remember, was repaid) my client showed a profit of $9,000 after two years, a return of almost $8,000 on the money she herself actually expended.

INVESTMENTS vs. INFLATION
How Investments Have Fared over the Past Decade

The record: $10,000 invested in stocks in 1968 would be worth about $10,310 today. Value in 1968 dollars, $5,460.

STOCKS

The record: Bonds of 10-year maturity bought at par for $10,000 in 1968 are now worth $10,000 when cashed in. Value in 1968 dollars, $5,297.

A BOND

The record: Each $10,000 invested in a new home in 1968 would be worth on the average about $22,200 on today's market. Value in 1968 dollars, $11,758

A HOME

The record: An investment of $10,000 in farmland in 1968 would be worth about $28,800 today. Value in 1968 dollars, $15,249.

FARMLAND

The record: For every $10,000 invested in an office building in 1968 today's value would be $21,580. Value in 1968 dollars, $11,430.

AN OFFICE BUILDING

The record: A study by Salomon Bros. shows these compound annual rates in the last decade: Chinese ceramics, 19.2%, gold, 16.3%, stamps, 15.4%, coins, 13%, diamonds, 12.6%, silver, 9.1%. Annual rate of rise in consumer price index, 6.8%.

COLLECTIBLES

Stockholders' Losing Battle

Stock market since World War II as measured by the Dow Jones average of industrial stocks, adjusted for changes in the cost of living—

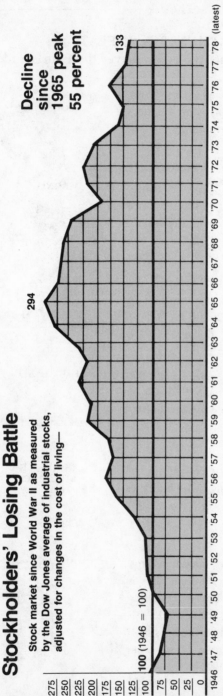

Decline since 1965 peak 55 percent

294

133

100 (1946 = 100)

275 250 225 200 175 150 125 100 75 50 25 0

1946 '47 '48 '49 '50 '51 '52 '53 '54 '55 '56 '57 '58 '59 '60 '61 '62 '63 '64 '65 '66 '67 '68 '69 '70 '71 '72 '73 '74 '75 '76 '77 '78 (latest)

Basic data Dow Jones & Company, U.S. Dept. of Labor

Investors who bought stocks since the mid-1950s that moved with the average generally find their portfolios worth less in purchasing power than what they paid. In the longer run, many stocks still are ahead.

On the bright side, dividends paid by corporations have averaged 4.5 percent a year since World War II, at least partially offsetting losses in portfolios' values.

Consider how much different the situation would have been if she had used her own money to invest. In her tax bracket, she'd have had to earn $7,700 to clear $5,000. Putting aside that kind of money would have meant crimping her lifestyle. And the return of $9,000 on that $7,700 would have been 11 percent—not bad, but far less impressive than the return using the bank's money. This technique is known as "leveraging," and it will be discussed in detail in a later chapter.

Leveraging, in this case, didn't increase the actual net gain from the investment. But it did allow my client to make a desirable investment without making a heavy cash commitment from her own resources. It left her free to pursue other potential investments—and the more like that one, the better!

Real estate is a good hedge against inflation. It is such an important investment topic that it will receive a chapter of its own. But it might be appropriate here to go into greater detail about some of the "doomsday investments" or hedges I mentioned earlier. Doomsday investments are investments in areas other than the traditional stocks and bonds. When investors are fearful of the economy, higher taxes, and decreased purchasing power of the dollar—to mention just a few of the economic factors that can alter one's style of living—they place their dollars in vehicles that have traditionally behaved in a manner contrary to stock market performance.

A recent study by the New York investment firm of Salomon Brothers shows just how well some of the finer collectibles have performed as investments since 1968. Even taking into account the effects of inflation, Chinese ceramics, diamonds, and collectible coins have appreciated from 12 to 19 percent, outstripping most of the traditional forms of investment. Gold is foremost among the "doomsday investments." Until just a few years ago, United States citizens couldn't own gold; according to United States law, only jewelers, dentists, and others who used it in business or manufacturing could purchase this precious element, and the price was controlled at $35 an ounce. When those laws were relaxed, however, there was a rush to buy gold on both the national and the international markets and the price quickly shot up to above $200 an ounce. The price underwent a decline, but during 1978 and 1979 the price of gold climbed inexorably—its rise matched by the decline of the dollar on world markets—and broke the $400-per-ounce barrier in the fall of 1979 and rose above $800 before 1979 ended.

Gold can be bought in several ways, but every method entails either a premium, a storage fee, or an appraisal fee. One means is to buy gold coins like the South African Krugerrand or the Austrian Kroner. You'll pay a premium for handling that will put the price somewhat above the actual value of that coin's weight in gold. Coin shops and some jewelry stores handle these coins, but be certain that you buy from a reputable dealer. That applies to all articles mentioned in the next few paragraphs, for the unhappy truth is that crooks will proliferate in any area where money is being made and deception is relatively simple.

Collectible coins offer another way of buying gold. The United States "double eagle" $20 gold piece is one example that offers the added bonus of a value to collectors beyond that of the gold it actually contains.

Gold can also be purchased in solid pieces ranging from quarter-ounce bits to 100-ounce bars. Many banks will handle the transaction. Once you've bought the gold, you have two alternatives: to take possesssion of the bars and store them yourself, or to accept a certificate that proves your ownership while the bars stay in a vault. The first choice has two drawbacks: You run the risk of theft unless the gold is securely stored, and you must pay an appraisal fee if you ever wish to sell the gold so that its weight and purity can be verified. Keeping the gold in the bank vault is safe and is proof of the gold's weight and quality when you put it up for sale, but some storage cost is involved.

The fourth way of taking advantage of the gold boom is to

buy a futures contract for gold on the commodities exchange market. Commodities contracts are explained in Chapter 7; they are a means of securing a promise that you will be able to buy a quantity of gold at a certain price on a certain date. It's not necessary for you actually to make the purchase. If the price of gold rises while you own the contract, the contract itself rises in value. That's a way to benefit from gold fever without ever owning any of the metal. There is a commission involved, and you should read carefully the sections of this book on options and commodities to understand the considerable risks inherent in these investments.

Silver is far more plentiful than gold and is much less expensive, but it also offers the same opportunities in the form of coins, bars, and commodity contracts. Silver's price has more than doubled in the last two years and, like the coffee contract illustration in Chapter 1, it rose dramatically and then declined in price just as fast as it had climbed. Like gold, silver is desirable because it has so many uses in industry and manufacturing.

Gemstones have proven to be a lucrative hedge in the last few years. In this field, however, you must be especially careful to deal only with reputable outlets. Diamonds seem to be a favorite haven for shysters and con men these days. Gems come in a multitude of grades according to their brilliance, their color, and the size of the imperfections, if any. These details will drastically influence the value of the stone, so it's important to be able to trust the dealer who grades the stones and sets the prices. Take some time to compare prices for different stones of the same grade. Be aware that you'll be paying a premium if you buy a stone at retail price and then try to sell it again, because at that point you'll be competing with the wholesale market. Rubies, emeralds, sapphires, topazes, aquamarines, and tourmalines are just some of the colored gem stones that have shown that they can more than hold their value during periods of high inflation.

Stamps can be a good investment, but you must be

selective. Only quality issues have increased appreciably in price. To be able to spot those stamps, you need to understand the field. Again, fakery is a definite possibility.

Paintings are much the same. Works by desirable artists show a predictable increase in value, but tastes change and you must keep current with them to protect yourself.

In the case of stamps, paintings, ceramics, statues, rare books, and other collectibles, you must have your collection appraised once a year and must keep your insurance updated to keep pace with what you hope will be the rising value of your collection. Photos of jewels, paintings, and stamps kept on file with your insurance agent will help facilitate any claim for theft.

Collectibles do not, as a rule, have the liquidity of an investment such as stocks or bonds. It is important to buy them only with money that would not be needed in an emergency.

5

WHERE TO PARK YOUR CASH WITH INTEREST

THERE are certain times when it is especially important to have ready cash, along with other investments you may have. I advocate having several months' reserve on hand for emergencies. In addition, however, cash is helpful during inflationary periods because inflation is almost always a harbinger of recession, and recession brings bargains both in investments and in personal purchases.

But you don't want inflation to eat away at the value of your cash. You want it at work, at least to hold its own against inflation's effects. This chapter, then, is a discussion of liquid assets—ready money—and the different ways you can put it to work for you while you decide how you're going to spend it.

To fall under this heading, a channel for your money must qualify on at least two counts: You must be assured of retaining at least the face dollar value of your money, and you must be able to put your hands on that money in a reasonable amount of time. Securities qualify under the second count, since you can immediately sell stocks, but there is no assurance that you will get back what you originally paid. On the other hand, you can be reasonably certain that a carefully chosen piece of improved real estate will hold its value (though there are no guarantees), but the money you put into real estate can't be easily retrieved under most circumstances. You must find a buyer, and the deal then must go through the lengthy escrow process.

But there are alternatives to simply putting your cash in a safe deposit box and letting its value deteriorate.

PASSBOOK ACCOUNTS

This is the basic bank savings account that for many small savers is the only obvious alternative to the checking account. Its advantage is that banks are plentiful and accessible; would-be savers daunted by brokerage house salespeople find the bank an easy-to-understand choice. But there is a price for that accessibility: Banks are currently paying 5 to 5.25 percent on passbook accounts; savings and loans pay .25 percent more. In addition, savings and loans now offer NOW (Negotiable Order of Withdrawal) accounts that allow the depositor to earn interest on money held in a checking account. It's important to read the small print in NOW account agreements, since most financial institutions demand that you keep a minimum balance on deposit in order to qualify for interest on checking. And if you've read the previous chapter, you know how disastrous these interest rates are to the value of your money in periods of 10 percent or even higher inflation.

You can find the same immediate liquidity with higher interest at thrift institutions. These concerns are not backed by the Federal Deposit Insurance Corporation, so there is some risk involved. They are free to invest their money in higher-risk speculations than regulated banks; these higher risks, as you know by now, mean both a higher possibility of failure and a higher potential rate of return. Thrift institutions pay up to 7.5 percent on passbook accounts. That's better than what banks can offer, but it's still not as good as other alternatives that actually carry less risk.

CERTIFICATES OF DEPOSIT

These are the banks' answer to those who seek a higher interest rate on their savings. Usually available in amounts of $1,000 or more, they offer rates that are higher than those of passbook savings accounts to savers who are willing to commit their money for periods that range from thirty days to eight years. It takes a substantial amount of money to get the highest rate: The longer the period, the greater the rate of interest. Certificates of deposit do offer immediate liquidity, since you can cash in the certificates at any time. But you will pay to exercise that option.

Probably you've heard certificates of deposit advertised in radio commercials. There's always a line added when interest rates are discussed: "Federal law requires substantial penalties for early withdrawal." Those penalties are, indeed, substantial—the loss of up to six months' interest, while the remaining interest reverts to what a standard passbook would have paid during the same period. In other words, if you wish to receive the advertised high interest, your money isn't really liquid at all.

You pay for the lack of flexibility in a couple of ways. You don't have the ready cash that you need, and in the event of rising inflation, you are locked into an interest rate that may be lower than what will be available later. Despite all this, the highest-paying certificates don't pay enough to keep up with high inflation.

If you have already bought certificates, and you find that you need immediate cash, you need to calculate the amount of money you will lose from the penalty if you withdraw and compare it to the cost of a loan for the remainder of the period during which your cash is committed. It's quite possible that it would make more sense to take out a loan to satisfy your cash needs and let the certificate come to maturity. The higher interest that you will earn from the matured certificate may more than cover the interest on the loan. (Most banks will lend up to 90 percent of the face value of a deposit certificate.)

CREDIT UNIONS

Many companies and corporations, large educational facilities, and even government-related work centers have credit unions. The credit union is composed of employees and their families, who deposit savings and can borrow against those savings to finance items such as a car or even a mortgage.

Because of the more stringent regulations they've faced in the past few years, credit unions now offer a more attractive alternative than they once did. In times of low inflation, their interest on savings—usually paid every ninety days in the form of a "dividend"—may be sufficient to offset the decreasing value of your money. Most also have available longer-term savings plans that pay higher rates of return, though your liquidity is restricted much as it is by the penalties on certificates of deposit.

One of the credit unions' pluses is that they offer loans and other services at rates lower than those of most banks. A good deal depends on the size of the credit union—the larger, the better. Federal credit unions usually are quite large and offer the most attractive rates for interest and services.

TREASURY BILLS

T-bills are issued on Monday morning by the Department of the Treasury in Washington, D.C. They are sold in $10,000 denominations. Like bonds, they are sold to mature at a given date—in this case, six months from the date of issuance. But unlike most bonds, they carry a rate of interest that is not fixed but is determined by auction when the bonds are issued. The weekly auction of T-bills is closely watched by financial analysts as a clue to the direction of the inflation rate. If the rate goes up significantly from one week to the next, analysts usually feel that the rate of inflation is headed up also. In the previous chapter I discussed the role that government spending plays in inflation. Since T-bills are issued to pay the day-to-day operating expenses of government, a rise in the interest rates set by the T-bill auction may be investors' way of making the government pay more for an increased demand for money.

Treasury *notes* are similar to Treasury bills except that they are issued for one-year terms and pay a slightly higher rate of interest. Treasury bonds—sometimes called "flower bonds" —are issued for five-year terms. The nickname derives from the unique way in which certain T-bonds can be used in estate planning. Because they mature immediately upon the death of the person in whose name they are issued, they often are bought in the name of a gravely ill person whose death is imminent. The bonds pay interest until death, and then the face value is used to pay estate taxes. Among the more affluent, they are said to be as common as flowers at the bedside of a dying relative. (Not all T-bonds qualify as flower bonds; you should check with a bond dealer to make sure.)

MONEY MARKET FUNDS

An understanding of money market funds begins with a grasp of what a mutual fund is. Basically, a mutual fund is a company or entity that uses its capital to invest in other companies. In the case of money markets, the capital or dollars may be yours, and it is used to invest in money related to other entities.

Money market funds were conceived several years ago during a period of high inflation to help small investors earn the higher interest available to those who had large sums of money for certificates of deposit, T-bills, and the like. Money markets are mutual funds of money, comprising top certificates of deposit from banks like Chase Manhattan and Bank of America, T-bills, T-notes, banker's acceptance loans that run for short terms (though longer than thirty days), and so-called commercial paper, day-to-day notes that pay extremely high rates of interest. The ordinary investor looking for a place to put cash used to have no access to sources like this. But the money market funds, with large amounts of cash at their disposal, have bought into all these sources. Because of the flexibility that their large assets afford them, they can allow certificates of deposit and T-notes to come to full term and thus earn maximum interest. They can produce large amounts of cash to buy commercial paper and other notes. As a result, money market funds pay interest rates comparable to those available a few years ago only to the most wealthy. Money market funds have paid interest in excess of 16.5 percent. The rate varies with inflation and the interest rates on short-term loans and Treasury bills.

There are a number of different funds, all of them instituted by mutual fund companies. Shares are sold at minimums ranging from $500 to $5,000. Interest is compounded. In addition, many funds offer check-writing privileges on the account. Shares earn interest until the checks arrive for collection. The only stipulations usually are that the checks be in amounts of at least $500 and that additional investments be no less than $100.

Brokerage houses and financial counselors carry prospectuses for the funds. The prospectus for each fund also can be obtained from the mutual fund company that offers the fund. (Most of these companies advertise regularly in the business sections of your local papers as well as in *The Wall Street Journal*.) The prospectus explains the goals, limitations, and rules of the fund, as well as the management fee involved. This is relatively low (from one-half to three-quarters of one percent in most cases), especially compared to the interest offered and the total liquidity that is the feature of all money market funds. Money market funds allow you to obtain your dollars whenever you need them, often by merely writing a check against your account.

The idea of money market funds hit banks and savings and loan institutions hard. Small investors by the droves closed out their passbook accounts, spurned certificates of deposit, and bought into money market funds. The financial institutions responded by offering money market certificates, similar to money market funds except that their interest is not compounded, they offer no check-writing privileges, and the minimum outlay is $10,000. There is no management fee, but—as with certificates of deposit—there is a penalty for pulling out of the certificate before it matures. This substantially reduces the practical liquidity of the money market certificates. Money market *funds*, however, remain perhaps the most attractive outlet for the small-to-medium investor looking for a good place to stash some cash.

(Sometimes there are practical matters that have to be taken into consideration. You may find it difficult to physically get to a bank or savings and loan to move your money to another institution. If that is the case, a phone call might move your money from a passbook or a mature certificate of deposit into a money market certificate. And remember that you should not take for granted that interest rates will always remain high on money market funds. Much depends on the current rate of inflation and the interest rate on T-bills and short-term loans. In January 1978, for example, bank passbook rates exceeded those offered by money market funds.)

Less sophisticated investors sometimes are dismayed to learn that money market funds are not insured by the Federal Deposit Insurance Corporation, as deposits in banks and savings and loans are. These people don't realize that the FDIC insurance is backed by the same institutions, like the Bank of America, whose certificates of deposit and loan acceptances form the backbone of money market funds. If huge banks like these should fail, then so, too, would the FDIC insurance. At that point we would all be in a great deal of trouble.

CASH VALUE OF LIFE INSURANCE

A high percentage of my new clients come into the office with life insurance policies that they have acquired in one of several common ways. Some of the policies were given as gifts and usually are of minimal cash value. Others were bought for them by their husbands as financial protection, or as investments, or as part of a divorce settlement. I tell these women that we will evaluate the policies just as we would any other investment. My advice to you is to follow the same practice if you are considering the purchase of a policy or are wondering what to do with an existing policy.

Remember that you are essentially a lender when you pay money into an insurance policy. You are paying money that the company is investing at a rate higher than the interest you are accumulating. So you must find out the interest rate that you are being paid, and you should know whether the company is paying regular dividends in any significant amount. Then, since we're talking about liquid assets, you have to know how much it will cost you to exercise that liquidity. In the case of life insurance that means "borrowing against the policy," though in fact you aren't borrowing at all but are merely getting back some of the money you already have put in. Most companies paid 3 percent interest, or slightly higher, until a couple of years ago, while charging 5 or 6 percent on money paid out. Recently those figures have climbed to 4 to 6 percent interest on accumulated cash, with 8 percent the usual charge for money paid out.

Find out what the specific figures are in your own case and then determine for yourself whether you wouldn't be better off cashing in the policy, buying term insurance (which may be cheaper), and putting your money to work somewhere else.

SECOND TRUST DEEDS

A second trust is a loan you have made to another person that is secured by a deed of trust against the borrower's real estate. These notes, for periods of one to five years, also seem to be popular among the women who come to my office for advice. The attraction is easy to understand. Where else can a woman make 10 percent and even higher interest so easily on a few thousand dollars?

But if you've read the chapter on inflation, you've seen just how bad a deal that seemingly attractive 10 percent can be. The main drawback is that the noteholder has no liquidity at all to speak of. The investment is committed for a certain period of time and can't be retrieved except on the off-chance that you are able to sell the note at a discounted price. Perhaps more important is the effect of high inflation on the value of the money that is lent out. The loan, when it matures, is paid back in dollars that are worth less than the original sum. The higher the rate of inflation, and the longer the term of the note, the more pronounced is the deterioration of the sum. Even the 10 percent rate of interest common with such notes isn't enough to offset the effects of high inflation, since that money is taxable. Thus, when you're considering whether to hold a note, you must weigh a number of factors, including the interest offered, the length of the note, the present rate of inflation, your own tax bracket, and the direction you expect the inflation rate to take during the term of the note. Be sure that you can afford to commit the money for that period of time. Since you are going to be assuming the role of a banker in this transaction, do it right, and ask for the credentials that any banker would require. Even though the note may be secured by a second deed of trust, the job of recovering the money through foreclosure and legal action is costly and time-consuming. Be certain that there is sufficient equity in the property after the first mortgage is satisfied to cover the amount you have lent. Just as a bank would, you should require a financial statement listing the borrower's salary, assets and liabilities, and place of employment. You need to be assured that the money will be promptly repaid. Let me emphasize that taking on a trust deed is serious business. If the owner of the property (the person to whom you have extended the note) should default on either the first or the second mortgage, you should be ready to assume, or "cure," the first mortgage to protect your own holdings. The only way to avoid this responsibility is to have a third note, the holder of which would have to "cure" both you and the holder of the first, to back you up. The interest rate on a deed of trust will vary according to the current mortgage rates and the general cost of money.

IOUs

I can think of no reason to lend money in IOUs except to help family members or close friends. To do so or not is your own decision. My advice in this case is twofold: First, lend out only as much money as you can afford to lose. You don't want to strain a relationship by being forced to demand money that you need from someone who can't afford to repay it. Second, make the transaction in the form of a standard note. That way, if the note comes due and isn't repaid, it can be claimed as a bad debt on your income taxes.

ANNUITIES

Some financial experts would argue that annuities aren't really liquid. But every one guarantees that all accumulated assets can be liquidated within seven days. That requirement satisfies my standard for liquidity.

Annuities are a life insurance product that have been popular with investors since the early part of this century. For years, annuities paid as little as 3.25 percent, but this was in a time when passbook accounts offered even less. Lately the interest has been upgraded. That is only part of annuities' attraction, however. It is their tax-favored treatment, under a policy known by the acronym FIFO, that accounts for much of their popularity with canny investors. Moreover, annuities (known in current terminology as single deferred annuities) are generally hedges against inflation, with an interest rate of about 9 percent, and are regarded by lenders as good collateral.

The tax advantages are twofold: Taxes are not charged on

money as it accumulates through interest, but only as it is withdrawn. This allows an investor to build up capital through interest while in her peak earning years and a high tax bracket, and to withdraw it during retirement when most taxpayers are in a lower bracket.

FIFO stands for the phrase, "First In, First Out." That's a reference to Internal Revenue Service policy, which states that early withdrawals, up to the amount of the original investment, are considered to come from that initial sum and are not taxable. An illustration: An investor puts $20,000 into an annuity, which then begins to accumulate interest. Five years later, she withdraws $10,000 from the account. That money—and the next $10,000 as well, any withdrawals up to $20,000—is considered to come from the first investment and is not taxed. In other words, the money that an investor first puts in is regarded as the same money that is first withdrawn. Thus, "First In, First Out."

Study the accompanying chart, which compares the income from $100,000 placed in a savings and loan account at 8.5 percent and an identical amount put into a typical annuity at 9 percent. Note that the interest accrued each year by the savings account is eaten away each year by taxes. Since we'll presume for this example that the investor is affluent, earning enough money to be in the 50 percent bracket, that portion consumed by taxes is rather large. This helps diminish the effect of compounding interest during the 10 years that the money stays in the account. At the end of this period, the interest is withdrawn each year, taxes are paid in the new 30 percent bracket (presuming that the investor now has retired), and the account keeps producing a steady but not especially large income that probably is worth less each year due to inflation's effects. Fourteen years into retirement, twenty-four years after the account is first instituted, the account shows a balance of $151,619, with $180,404 having been paid out in interest. But once the IRS has taken its 30 percent share of that figure, the spendable income over a fourteen-year period becomes $126,280.

SAVINGS AND
LOAN ACCOUNTS
vs. DEFERRED
ANNUITIES:
$100,000
ILLUSTRATION

FOR: 0000
SEX: F
Report No. CMMG623T   RET.AGE: 65

Assuming

1. You can earn 8.50 percent in a taxable account and 9.05 percent in a deferred annuity.
2. In each example you allow the funds to accumulate for ten years.
3. During that accumulation period taxes are calculated at 50 percent.
4. After year 10 taxes are calculated at 30 percent.
5. After year 10 you withdraw all interest income from the taxable account pay taxes (30 percent).
6. After year 10 in the deferred annuity you withdraw an average of 7.00 percent of original principal once per year. (Our further assumption is that these withdrawals are "irregular" in frequency and therefore are considered to be return of principal and non-taxable.) If the withdrawals are "regular" in frequency they may be taxable. Withdrawals in excess of original principal will definitely be taxable as income.

END OF YEAR	TAXABLE ACCOUNT	DEFERRED ANNUITY
START	$100,000	$100,000
1	$104,250	$109,050
2	$108,682	$118,920
3	$113,302	$129,680
4	$118,117	$141,420
5	$123,136	$154,210
6	$128,367	$168,170
7	$133,824	$183,350
8	$139,511	$199,990
9	$145,439	$218,090
10	$151,619	$237,830

END OF YEAR	BAL-ANCE	TAXABLE INTEREST	AFTER TAX SPEND-ABLE $	BAL-ANCE	AFTER TAX SPENDABLE $
	$151,619			$237,831	
11	$151,619	12,886	9020	252,352	7000
12	151,619	12,886	9020	268,194	7000
13	151,619	12,886	9020	285,466	7000
14	151,619	12,886	9020	304,304	7000
15	151,619	12,886	9020	324,843	7000
16	151,619	12,886	9020	347,238	7000
17	151,619	12,886	9020	371,659	7000
18	151,619	12,886	9020	398,298	7000
19	151,619	12,886	9020	427,344	7000
20	151,619	12,886	9020	459,015	7000
21	151,619	12,886	9020	493,554	7000
22	151,619	12,886	9020	531,225	7000
23	151,619	12,886	9020	572,299	7000
24	151,619	12,886	9020	617,092	7000
	$151,619	$180,404	$126,280	$617,092	$98,000

$465,473 MORE!

ANNUAL ANNUITY PAYOUTS AT RETIREMENT AGE

10 Years certain & Life	57,612
20 Years certain & Life	47,985
Life only	63,240

*There is no assurance that this rate will be maintained during the accumulation period.

**Assumes current annuity rates based on the total assumed accumulation which may or may not apply at the time the annuity payments commence.

***Withdrawals (during the accumulation period) in excess of original principal will definitely be taxable as income.

You can see what a difference the tax-favored status of the annuity makes. By the end of the first year alone, the annuity has accumulated almost $5,000 more than the savings and loan account. By the end of five years, the difference has grown to almost $21,000. At the end of ten years, the gap is more than $86,000.

The differences after the tenth year, when the investor drops into a 30 percent bracket and begins to withdraw money, are even greater.

After year 10, the investor takes about 7 percent of the original investment each year, $7,000 while the interest continues to compound in the annuity. Because of the FIFO policy, that income is considered to come from the original investment and thus is not taxed. By the end of the twenty-fourth year, the annuity has grown to $617,092 and has paid $98,000 in nontaxed income.

Now the advantages really begin to show. After the twenty-fourth year, the savings account holder can either spend the $151,619 in the account or can continue to draw a steady interest that is continually diminished by inflation. But the annuity holder can either cash in—a whopping $617,000—or can annuitize the amount. In so doing, she gives up her right to cash out the whole amount but is guaranteed large payments for as long as she lives.

Actually, there are several choices. The investor can choose to annuitize for "life only," to use the companies' term. That means that the company guarantees to pay a set amount each year for the rest of her lifetime. That amount varies according to the investor's age and is determined by the insurance company's mortality tables. Thus, if she should live longer than the company expects, the investor will receive payments totaling even more than the $617,092. In any event, the payments will be quite large.

There are two other options that might be more attractive to an investor who wishes to leave an estate to her heirs. She could decide to take a "ten-year certain," which means that payments will be made either to the investor or to her heirs for at least ten years. If the investor lives longer, she will continue to receive the sum for life. Because of the "certain" feature, the payout sum is slightly smaller than the "life only" payout.

Another alternative is "twenty years certain," which guarantees annual payouts to the investor or to the beneficiaries for at least twenty years, and longer, if the investor should survive that period. Again, because of the assurance that the money will be paid for twenty years, whether the annuity holder lives or not, the payout is substantially lower than either "life only" or "ten years certain and life."

Annuities have other attractive features. Insurance companies generally follow conservative fiscal practices and are bound by law to carry adequate reserves, which makes them even steadier than banks in times of severe economic depression. During the Depression fifty years ago, only 2 percent of insurance companies failed. The attrition rate for banks was above 30 percent.

Annuities, like life insurance, also bypass probate, thus eliminating court and attorney costs, and the beneficiaries can be easily changed.

Some insurance companies even offer a rider to the policy that stipulates that the interest rate on the account will increase if rates go up during the period of accumulation.

You can buy annuities from an insurance agent. I recommend, however, that you deal not with an agent representing a single company, but with an independent broker who deals in the products of several companies. Each company offers significantly different features; some annuities are better buys than others. Look for the guarantees of each annuity, and the commission. Find out the penalties involved if you should wish to get out of the account during the accumulation period. Some companies have penalties that seem to go on forever; others penalize on a declining scale that ends after the first six years.

6

HOW TO GET AND USE CREDIT

IN an earlier chapter, I mentioned that in any unstable economy, such as one that would be caused by inflation, there will be a great many people adversely affected by the disruption and a fortunate few who will have the insight and the expertise to take advantage of the situation. Many economists are seeing another reflection of this in the field of credit and borrowing. The availability of money for credit is always limited. Some people will use their credit foolishly. Others will not get the full advantage of the credit to which their net worth and earning power entitle them. Some will pay higher interest rates than they must, while lenders charge lower rates to more canny borrowers. Only a few will use their credit to its maximum without extending themselves too far. You can join that select group of aware, sophisticated borrowers who use their assets to best advantage.

The object of this book is to help you increase your net worth by use of sound money management and a cogent financial plan. Credit, borrowing, and "leverage"—a term I'll define shortly—ought to be an indispensable part of that plan. We can safely assume that very few of us have at our immediate disposal all the cash we need not only to live well, but to make all the investments we want to make so as to increase our net worth and stay ahead of the effects of inflation.

We do, however, have credit and leverage.

Credit is an inescapable part of modern life. The fact is that we rarely have enough money to pay immediately for every material thing that we want to buy. But in a healthy economy, most of us can count on having money coming in regularly. Credit is extended to us on that assumption, with the expectation that we will pay our debts with the money that will be ours in the future.

Leverage is the calculated use of that credit so that we use other people's money to make money for ourselves. Of course, it's possible to overdo that. You never want to borrow so much money that the payments to meet your obligations every month exceed the income that you have available to make these payments. In a way, using maximum leverage is like walking to the edge of a canyon to get a better view of the river below. The closer you get to the edge, the better . . . until you take one step too many. If you find that, after you have adjusted your withholding taxes to increase your monthly cash flow and have identified all other possible sources of income, you are unable to meet monthly cash flow needs, then you are over-leveraged.

You'll find that "leverage" is an extremely apt word if you remember anything from high school physics. A lever is a device that allows you to exert effort beyond the actual force that you use. You can use a lever to lift an object that you ordinarily wouldn't be able to budge. Leverage in the financial sense means that you're able to purchase things you ordinarily wouldn't be able to afford, using only assets on hand. If it is used wisely, leverage can work to accelerate the growth of your net worth. A couple of quick examples illustrate the point.

For the first, we'll take the mythical $100,000 home that I like to talk about. We'll assume that you have the $20,000 cash necessary for a normal down payment. Your financial report satisfies a bank, which advances you the other $80,000 you need to buy the house. You, in return, pay the bank interest on the money you are using and gradually pay off the principal amount you owe.

That itself is simple leverage. But let's take it a step further and assume not only that you are able to convince the bank to lend you $80,000 but also that you have a second source willing to put up an additional $10,000. You use that as part of your down payment on the home, which leaves you $10,000 in your savings account.

Assume that you hold the property for three years, then sell it for $150,000. Fees and commissions will reduce that sum to $138,000. Subtract from that the $80,000 you owe the bank (since the principal will have been reduced very little in just three years), subtract another $10,000 which you repay to your generous second lender, and subtract the other $10,000 which you yourself put up in the deal. Your profit is $38,000 from an initial outlay of just $10,000 from your own resources, a net return of 380 percent over three years.

If you had not borrowed the additional $10,000 your outlay would have been $20,000. The return on your $20,000 would be $38,000, or 190 percent.

So far, this is just juggling figures, because the eventual cash out is the same in either case. But suppose, after borrowing from a second lender to make half your down payment, you took the $10,000 that was left over in your accounts and put it to work for you in another such profitable investment. Perhaps you used it as a 20 percent down payment on a second home costing $50,000. You use the rental income from this second home to cover most of the mortgage payments. If it, like the first home, appreciates 50 percent in three years, it will be worth $75,000 when you dispose of it. Even with the fees and commissions on this other house, you will still show a handsome profit of perhaps $20,000 on this second $10,000 investment. Now leverage has really begun to work for you. In all three cases, you started with the same $20,000 cash in an account. In the first instance, where you used that full amount as a down payment, your profit from the single home after three years is

$38,000. You have used only part of the credit available to you. But in the final case, leverage has been used to the maximum. You are leveraged not only in the original $80,000 loan from the bank, but in the $10,000 borrowed from the second lender and in the $40,000 mortgage taken out to pay for the second home. The profit is perhaps $58,000 instead of $38,000, though in each instance the sum of capital was the same.

The advantage of leverage is even more dramatically illustrated in another example. I've said that the art of leverage is in using credit to the maximum without exceeding your ability to make payments on your debts. In this case, the income from rental of property provides most of that means, and the tax advantages from payment of interest will be presumed to cover the rest. These projections, plus the fact that their investment will be protected by the 20 percent down payment on the property, convinces the banks to lend a rather substantial amount of money.

Let's say that a woman with $100,000 to invest buys outright a single home worth that sum. There is no mortgage. She is not leveraged at all. It is safe to project that the property will appreciate at 10 percent per year, and you can follow the progress of the home's value in the accompanying chart. After a year, the property is worth $110,000 ($100,000 plus 10 percent of $100,000). After the second year, the value is $121,000 ($110,000 plus 10 percent of $110,000). After five years, the value of the property has increased to $159,841. If the woman sells at the end of the five-year period, she shows a profit of $59,841, or approximately 59 percent.

But suppose, instead of buying a single house for $100,000, she uses that money for four down payments of $20,000 each on homes costing $100,000. Instead of one home increasing in value at 10 percent a year, she has four homes, each one originally valued at $100,000 and each one increasing at 10 percent a year. The fifth $20,000 can be used as a reserve.

By the end of the first year alone (see chart), her equity in the four homes totals $40,000, nearly two-thirds the value of the single home after five years. By the end of the second year, her equity in the four homes equals $84,000. By the end of the fifth year, when she sells the homes at their inflated price of $159,000 apiece, her equity in the four homes has climbed to $239,364. Subtract from that the original $100,000 stake of capital, and you'll find she is left with $139,364 in pure profit, a return of 139 percent on her original stake.

Or put it in terms of the inflation that seems to be with us perpetually. Over five years, the $59,840 profit from that single house has barely offset the effects of 10 percent inflation on the original $100,000. But four homes have provided a profit as well as a hedge against inflation.

For illustration purposes, I have not allowed for a small reduction in the mortgage due to the great proportion of monthly payments that is allotted to interest in the first few years. Real estate agents' commissions have not been deducted, nor have the tax advantages from interest payments, real estate taxes, expenses and depreciation been included. In real estate investments, one of the greatest areas of tax advantage comes from depreciation. To the investor and taxpayer this could mean a great reduction in tax obligations, making the rate of return even greater than the illustration shows.

$100,000 REAL ESTATE INVESTMENT—TWO WAYS
$100,000

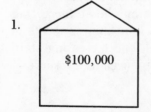

1.

$100,000

All cash—increasing by
10 percent/year
Year 1: $110,000;
Year 2: $121,000;
Year 3: $132,100;
Year 4: $145,310;
Year 5: $159,841

2.

Increasing at 10% per year

	Market Value	Mortgage	Equity
Year 1: 4 houses @ $110,000 =	$440,000	$320,000	$120,000
2: 4 houses @ $121,000 =	$484,000	$320,000	$164,000
3: 4 houses @ $132,100 =	$528,400	$320,000	$208,000
4: 4 houses @ $145,310 =	$581,240	$320,000	$261,240
5: 4 houses @ $159,841 =	$639,364	$320,000	$319,364

	Investment 1	Investment 2
Current market value:	$159,841	$639,364
Increased dollar value over initial $100,000:	$ 59,841	$219,364
Percentage increase:	59.8%	219.3%

The idea of using another's money to make a profit can be applied over a shorter period of time, a few days instead of years. Banks have made an art of it. This is called "float," and if you have a checking account or a passbook savings account, some of the money being used is your own.

Although money deposited into a checking account can be drawn out immediately, it rarely is. Usually the money is paid out to honor checks over a period of several days or weeks. The money accumulated in the thousands of checking accounts carried by a major bank is always enormous. Since the bank reasons that all the money is never paid out at any one time, and since the bank has reserves to make the payment if that unlikely occurrence actually should happen, it has at its disposal hundreds of thousands of dollars that can be lent on a short-term basis for high interest. The money that is repaid goes back into the checking pool. The very volume of money handled guarantees a certain stability and flexibility; meanwhile, a percentage of the money in the checking pool is always being lent at a high interest rate. You deposit money into your account, and the bank promises that it will return the money any time you request it by writing a check. But your money doesn't sit there. It goes into the pool, and the dollars you get back by writing a check aren't necessarily the same dollars you put in. Banks make sure that no more money than necessary is ever sitting around doing nothing, even overnight. (That ought to be a hint to you when you formulate your own financial strategy.)

This process is most obvious in the common banking practice of "holding" an out-of-town check until it clears the bank on which it is written. You may have been through this if you've ever tried to deposit a check at a bank with which you don't have a strong working relationship. You may deposit the check, you're told, but you won't be able to draw on the funds for at least a week, until the check clears.

In modern banking, that process rarely requires more than a couple of days. Even during that two-day period, the funds aren't just sitting idle. They've gone into the pool. (One well-known California bank has become notorious for this practice, holding funds up to ten days.)

Inflation allows you to turn float to your own advantage if you do a little creative planning of your purchases. Find out the billing cycle of your credit cards (there is usually a notation that reads "Billing period," or "Charge and payments received after . . . will be billed next month," and is constant from month to month). Then, if you are about to make a major purchase, wait until just after the billing date.

Your purchase will not appear until the next month's bill, four weeks away. Wait until a week before the end of the billing period to send in your check to cover the purchase. You have just taken advantage of seven weeks of "float," which allows you to pay off the debt in money that has been devalued by seven weeks' worth of inflation. And, as this is written, that can amount to as much as 2 percent, or $20 on a $1,000 purchase. A couple of such purchases can more than pay for the annual cost of a national credit card. It's far smarter than paying 18 percent on a bank card, since inflation has yet to reach those heights.

By now you ought to have some idea of what leverage is and how it can work for you. Maybe you're convinced that keeping dollars idle is a terribly wasteful practice, especially during inflationary times. Now you want to go borrow. What you encounter when you sit down with a loan officer at a bank depends almost entirely on your credit background and your earning power. Unfortunately, many women fall short of the ideal in both areas.

It is far beyond the scope of this book to enumerate the problems that women face in the job market when they ask to be paid the same as men for performing an identical job. But it is very much a concern of this book that you receive all the credit you deserve according to your earning background and your credit history.

Until a few years ago, almost no woman could expect to be treated the same as a man when she applied for a loan. When a married couple applied for a loan—especially a mortgage— bank officers routinely disregarded or else sharply discounted the wife's salary when evaluating their ability to assume debt. It was assumed that the woman would very shortly be quitting work to stay home and have children. That assumption was unfair from the beginning. Now it is also usually erroneous and quite illegal.

Women sometimes paid higher interest rates than men, on the unfounded rationale that women were poor credit risks. A woman with high income often was required to have her husband's cosignature when applying for a loan, even though in some cases she made more money than he did.

This began to change in January 1975, with a reform of the community property laws in the eight states that subscribe to the community property practice: California, Idaho, Louisiana, New Mexico, Nevada, Arizona, Texas, and Washington. Until that time, the husband was considered to have control of the community property (defined as the income of both husband and wife during their marriage, and any increase in the value of their earnings and properties due to their labor during the marriage). Women often were denied loans without their spouses' signatures, because creditors could attach only the husband's income, not the wife's.

The reform of the law meant that husband and wife had equal control of community property, thus giving creditors access to both incomes. The husband's signature was no longer required. This, in turn, led to the 1977 Equal Credit Opportunity Act, which established some essential rights for women in credit. One of these restricts any lender's inquiry about the woman's marital status to just three choices: married, single, or separated—and this is only in the community property states, where the spouse's income and debts are the responsibility of both parties. The act also stipulated that a woman's income had to be given the same consideration as a man's when the two were applying for a loan together. A woman now is entitled to claim child support and alimony payments as income on a financial statement, as long as she can prove that the payments are being made regularly.

Most important, the act gave women the chance to get equal recognition for bills promptly paid and accounts well maintained. They were allowed to have their names entered with those of their husbands on all joint charge accounts. This is important because it enables women to establish a credit history and identity of their own. Women who had been paying the family bills for years were shocked to find when they were widowed or divorced that as "Jane Smith" they had no standing with any credit bureau. They were known only as "Mrs. Bob Smith," if they were known at all.

Unfortunately, the public response to the act was poor. Relatively few women have taken the opportunity to get equal recognition for the family's good credit.

My advice to you is to shop around for a loan just as you would for any other commodity that comes with different features at different prices. Tell bank loan officers that you are doing comparison shopping. I've found that smaller, community-oriented banks may charge up to 2 percent less than large banks for an otherwise identical loan. Credit unions will almost always charge less than banks. A bank may offer you a lower interest charge in return for all your banking business, which is fair enough. But interest rates aren't the only factor to be considered. Find out whether you are eligible for free services that you would use and for which you would be charged elsewhere: cashier's checks, your regular checking account, traveler's checks. Find out whether the bank will be willing to cover an overdrawn check for a few days if there is money in a savings account to back it up.

You also ought to find out what the limits of that particular branch may be. Is it equipped to handle quickly and efficiently the business you bring it? You may be involved with situations that require recurrent borrowing; how large a loan can the local officers approve on their own? If the application has to be handed over to a central loan officer, you might have to wait several weeks to get an answer—too long, in many cases.

Finally, you'll be doing yourself a favor if you acquaint yourself with the different kinds of loans that the bank offers, the different down payments, and the interest rates that go with each. Most banks offer different kinds of loans for homes, cars, boats, travel, and education. Many bankers themselves aren't aware of all the loans that are available and the special features of each.

One loan that you want to avoid at all costs is the so-called consolidation loan. Banks don't offer this kind of services, which means that you'll be going to a finance company.

First, if you have so many financial problems that you actually need such a loan, you should immediately tear up your credit cards and begin to live on a cash-only basis as a first step to recovering.

Second, you could find yourself paying as much as 30 percent interest for such a loan because of the way the finance companies structure the payoff. The loans are set up so that you pay mostly interest in the first few months of the loan. Then if you should feel after a few months that you are ready to pay off the loan, you'll discover that you have been paying mostly interest and that you've made little dent in the principal, although the life of the loan may be very short.

With the laws now protecting women in the credit field, you ought to be judged the same way as a man would be when you apply for a loan. That means that the credit report that any lender will order is going to be essential. I mentioned these reports earlier. The reporting agency is likely to carry such information as your salary, past and present employment, address, and Social Security number. It may list many of the accounts in your name, the date on which they were opened, whether you are late or current with payments, your highest balance, and your current balance. Any negative report can be carried seven years; bankruptcy will be carried for fourteen years. And, as I discussed earlier, if a negative report is issued against you, you have the right to find out the nature of that report, to dispute it if you feel it is unfair, and to have the mistake corrected and your creditors notified of the error.

If you feel that you have been treated unjustly, there are a number of agencies to which you can turn, depending on the business with which you have been dealing.

If you have a complaint against any retail store, consumer finance company, or nonbank creditor, contact the Federal Trade Commission.

For state chartered savings and loans, go to the state Savings and Loan Department.

For federally chartered savings and loans, go to the Home Loan Bank of your area.

If you have a complaint against any state-chartered credit union, industrial loan companies, or finance companies, seek the help from your state's Department of Corporations.

If you are unhappy with the treatment you receive from any credit union, contact one of the regional directors of the National Credit Union Administration.

For nationally chartered banks (these can be identified by the word "National" in their names), go to the officer or controller of currency.

For state-chartered banks, go to the state's Department of Banking, usually located in the capital city.

For banks that are members of the Federal Reserve System, deal directly with whatever Federal Reserve bank is closest to you. (There are only twelve.)

The state attorney general's office will deal with many serious credit problems.

Additional information about the Equal Opportunity Credit Act can be obtained from the Federal Reserve System, Washington, D.C. 20551.

Almost any of the agencies named above can help direct

you to the proper channel for your complaint. Also, many cities and states have consumer protection agencies that are helpful clearinghouses for information about credit abuse.

7

INVESTMENTS (1): STOCKS, BONDS, AND COMMODITIES

You should have no trouble understanding the stock market if you can see in your mind's eye a large open-air bazaar: hundreds of booths displaying a myriad of goods and wares (some bargains, some overpriced), constant haggling between buyer and seller, with all the business conducted in an atmosphere of confusion that is impenetrable to all but the best-informed. The stock market is a lot like that.

If that image doesn't come so readily to mind, you might picture a glittering Las Vegas casino that offers a dozen games of chance, each with its own nuances and subtleties. Imagine players winning great amounts of money (sometimes all betting on the same roll of the dice). Imagine the majority of people walking away losers, with only a special few managing to beat the house consistently. The stock market is a lot like that, too.

There's much truth in both analogies. The stock market is, in fact, a bazaar. For six hours every day, the New York Stock Exchange (the major exchange) is a frantic, nonstop auction during which buyers bid simultaneously on thousands of different securities and bonds. The action is hectic and sometimes baffling to an outsider, but there is no better way to understand the way the market moves than to watch the bidding on a hot stock. Five minutes on the floor of the exchange is proof that the market is a very human activity, subject to human whims and excitements and depressions. That built-in unpredictability is one of its attractions.

There is, as well, an undeniable element of gambling, with all the rapid success and failure of a fast-moving dice game. Action on the stock market is only slightly less immediate than what you'll find at a dice table. That, too, is one of the market's big attractions. The comparison holds up even one step further. In the market, just as at a casino craps game, it's always possible to make money. A pessimistic investor can profit from a downturn in the market just the way a gambler playing a hunch can make money during a cold streak at the tables. History bears this out; even in the most dismal months of the Depression, there was money being made in the market.

And to carry the analogy one last step: Just as in a casino, there are dozens of ways to invest money in the stock market. But laying money out blindly is inviting disaster. Unlike the craps player, you don't have to rely on luck in the stock market. However, you must know the rules and you must be able to make an intelligent decision about where and when to invest your cash.

Therefore, this chapter will necessarily be a long one. In truth, there are more important places to invest, based on the stock market's recent performance. It's quite possible to plan a successful financial strategy without buying a single bond or a solitary share of stock. Still, few investors ever pass up the market completely. The lure is simply too great.

For one thing, the market is symbolic of our entire economic system. With the possible exception of home owning (which has only recently become a true investment, with all that the word implies), it is our most popular form of speculation. And when you've truly grasped the mysterious workings of the market, then you'll probably also have a sound basic understanding of the principles of investment and money management.

Sooner or later, as you execute your financial plan, you will want to try the market. I encourage you to do so when you feel that you are ready and the market is right. It is potentially rewarding, and almost always exciting. Before you wager a single dollar in that big casino, though, you'll need to understand all the games and how they're played.

Once you've got a good overview of the market, and you've sampled the different ways money can be invested in the market, you may want to specialize in one particular field. The one you choose will depend as much on your personality as on your financial position. Some people are attracted by a fast-moving commodities contract that can be affected drastically by weather, politics, consumer tastes, and even fear of inflation, as in the case of gold. Others will feel more comfortable with a sedate and relatively inactive bond, far less subject to wide fluctuations in value.

The point is that it's feasible to sample many of the market's different facets, either alone or in partnership with friends. That is one of its selling points—its accessibility for the small investor. You can start with a small investment and, if you've done your homework, you can have the same opportunity as the manager of a multimillion-dollar trust fund. That's because of another selling point that attracts me even more: All the information necessary to make an intelligent investment decision about the market is easily available to everyone. I'm convinced that there are places in the market where the novice investor willing to do some hard work in preparation can outperform the vast majority of professionals.

Most new investors will be working with limited funds. In the market, at least, that's not a crippling handicap. Small investors still have a place in the market, though brokers naturally prefer to handle accounts with six-figure portfolios. One brokerage firm, Merrill Lynch, has a plan that allows small investors to buy full and fractional shares of stocks listed on the New York and American Exchanges, as well as 550 over-the-counter stocks, with investments as small as $20 a month. And the National Association of Investment Clubs (1515 E. Eleven Mile Rd., Royal Oak, Mich., 48067) has a similar investment plan with a smaller selection of stocks.

THE EXCHANGES

The stock market as we know it was formed in New York in 1792. It was an auction market, conducted beneath a buttonwood tree. Businessmen gathered to sell and trade their shares of ownership in companies, most of them railroad companies. A few hundred shares traded was considered a busy day. Business was conducted by gentlemen's agreement. Sellers of stock weren't required to have the certificates in their possession, and bidders could purchase stock without immediately producing cash.

Though the business is conducted on a far larger scale now, those two essential elements remain. The market is still an auction, with prices established purely by means of supply and demand. And, by necessity, the gentleman's agreement still holds. To operate otherwise would hopelessly impede the millions of transactions that are conducted each week on the floors of the exchanges. Traders on the floor every day buy and sell thousands of shares which they never see. And when you have established an account with your broker, you will be able to order the purchase of securities or bonds or options simply on the promise that the money to cover those purchases will be arriving within a few days in the brokerage house's office or branch.

Today, the business of the stock market is conducted on two major national exchanges: the New York Stock Exchange (NYSE) and the American Stock Exchange (AMEX), both located in New York City. Each exchange sets standards for the companies that wish to have their stock listed on that exchange. The NYSE is the stricter of the two, with tough requirements for a proven earnings record and demonstrated financial stability. In addition, the two exchanges both set stringent requirements for notifying stockholders of the financial condition of the firms in which they hold stock. This is done with periodic reports.

Several large cities, such as Chicago and San Francisco, have their own exchanges, on which regional and local stocks are traded. Finally, there is an over-the-counter market for stocks in companies that do not yet qualify for listing on an exchange, or that choose not to be listed. These stocks are traded within brokerage houses. The over-the-counter market was risky business until recently. Price quotations were often as much as two hours late and could be several points different from the true trading price as a result of that discrepancy. But modern quotation systems have largely ended that problem, and the over-the-counter market is now a feasible avenue for investment.

Because of its stringent regulations, the NYSE is considered the most solid and most prestigious of the exchanges. A company will be dropped from the listing if it fails to maintain the NYSE standards for earnings, stability, and reporting. Occasionally, a company that has been dropped from the listing will requalify. The AMEX, because of its somewhat less strict requirements, is somewhat less highly regarded. The over-the-counter market is the logical starting point for new companies, which lack the past performance record to qualify for listing on the exchanges.

I recommend a tour of a major exchange. The NYSE offers scheduled tours that include an explanation of the exchange and its history, with a look at the floor itself. The floor is dotted with stations, or booths, that house traders specializing in certain groups of stocks. Each stock traded on the exchange is represented somewhere on the floor. Bids and offerings both are handled through that station, with members of all the major brokerage houses executing orders to buy and sell just as they are received in the houses and are transmitted to the floor. These orders are logged in at a specific time, and the current trading price is noted along with it. (This provides an important backup system for settling disputes between brokers and customers, as we'll see later.) The system works well. It is far more orderly than we might expect it to be, given the huge volume of shares traded every day.

SECURITIES

Securities—common or preferred stock—represent partial ownership in a company. By issuing and publicly offering shares for sale, a corporation is dividing ownership into a set number of equal portions. The number is determined by the charter or by-laws of the corporation, and in the case of a large national company, a single share truly is partial ownership, possibly .0001 percent, or less. That intangible ownership is represented by a piece of paper—a stock certificate that bears the name of the company, the number of shares, the name of the stockholder, and the date of issuance. (That traditional method is somewhat cumbersome, given the millions of shares traded each week, and there is general talk in the industry that the certificates may be replaced by computer cards.)

A company may issue stock for a number of reasons, most of which can be reduced to a single one—the need to raise capital. You may imagine this on the small scale of a neighborhood grocery that needs money to expand its building and buy new fixtures. Lacking the money to make the improvements, the sole owner agrees to sell a certain percentage—perhaps 25 percent—of his business to an outsider in return for the money needed. The improvements are completed. The new partial owner now shares one-quarter of the risks and rewards of that business. The original owner has surrendered part of the business. But if he has calculated the improvements shrewdly, his 75 percent of the expanded business is even more valuable than 100 percent of what the store had been previously.

Some companies may issue stock to employees as a way of reducing or eliminating salaries, thus keeping overhead down and increasing the amount of capital that can now be used for other purposes. Walt Disney did this once, in the early years of his new production company, and those employees who accepted stock and a reduced salary did very well as the company grew and the stock became more valuable.

The effects of this stock-sharing plan are especially notice-able in a one-industry "company town" that depends on a single company to employ much of its work force. Forest City, Iowa, is the site of a manufacturing plant for the company that produces Winnebago motor homes, a company that made its stock readily available to employees at all levels. Stock in Winnebago has risen and dropped sharply at least twice in the last six years as sales of motor homes have been affected by gasoline availability, and a significant portion of Forest City's populace, shareholders in the com-pany, has become richer or poorer (at least on paper) with each fluctuation.

I mentioned earlier that ownership of stock means sharing in the risks and the rewards of the company. The risk is limited to the amount you've paid for the stock. You could lose every penny if the company fails. (I'll discuss later what happens to stockholders when a company goes bankrupt.) The rewards can take several forms. First, if the company's earnings increase, the stock tends to become more attractive, raising the price of each share. Taking advantage of that reward, though, requires selling the stock. Or, a company can issue a dividend: In effect, it takes some of the profits made during the last accounting period and returns them to the shareholders, the partial owners, of the company. A series of dividends also tends to make the stock itself more valuable, especially to potential buyers seeking an income from their investment.

Directors of a company, however, usually are quite reluc-tant to part with cash profits. They would generally prefer to use the money for expansion, improvements, and capital investments. Since they are aware that stockholders want some benefit from stock in a profitable company, they might decide to reduce or eliminate the cash dividend and issue more stock to the holders of the existing stock. This is a common practice of young companies that need capital for growth.

One of your rights as a stockholder is the opportunity to

attend annual shareholders' meetings. Here the stock-holders, the owners of the company, are given the chance to participate in important company matters. Most important of these is the election of a board of directors that will be responsible for specific corporate affairs. If you're unable to attend a meeting and vote in person, you have the right to receive a proxy card and vote by mail, throwing your shares with the faction that supports the slate of your choice. If there are serious philosophical differences within the corporate structure, stockholders may find themselves in a proxy fight, with different candidates each requesting your proxy support.

Stockholders have the right to receive quarterly reports on the financial condition of the company, as well as more comprehensive annual reports. These annuals can be very instructive, especially when considered along with the reports for the past several years. Simply by comparing the figures from one year to the next, you can get a good idea of what the company is doing by seeing how and where its income is being disbursed.

In recent years there has been a tendency for companies to buy up as many shares of their common stock as possible. Often this will happen if the company's directors feel that the stock is undervalued. Buying up the stock on the open market naturally creates a higher demand, which forces up the price of the stock to more reasonable levels. Of course, this benefits those shareholders who retain their stock. On paper, at least, their holdings are more valuable. And the higher market price means that the company can set a higher par value if it should create a new issue of common stock. (Par value merely means a dollar amount that is assigned to a common share by a company's charter. It does not reflect the true value of the shares.) Furthermore, buying up the shares means that the company need pay out less of its profits in dividends. On top of all this, the lower number of shares makes the company's earning ratio seem more impressive.

This, in turn, tends to make the outstanding stock even more attractive to potential buyers.

There is an additional side benefit: By retreating from the public sector back into private ownership, a company frees itself from the regulations of the exchanges and of the federal Securities Exchange Commission. The company is relieved of the responsibility for quarterly and annual reports and stockholders' meetings, major entries in the expense budget of any large public corporation.

My point in mentioning all this is to show some of the outside influences that can cause considerable fluctuation in the price of a stock. As a potential investor, you should be aware of what can happen to your holdings when the company in which you own stock either acquires, or is acquired by, another company. Tenders, acquisitions, and mergers have a definite effect not only on the stock in the company being acquired but also on the stock of the acquiring company.

Such dealings are quite common today, as large corporations try to diversify and branch out into other fields that aren't related to the main area of their own business. This is desirable so that a catastrophe in one specific area is partially offset by the profits from other areas that aren't affected by the failure.

Avon cosmetic company was once considered one of the most successful concerns in its field. The company had a virtual corner on the market of door-to-door cosmetic sales, and the market was a large one. Avon salespeople could count on a potential customer's coming to the door of almost every home they visited. But Avon's success naturally spawned competitors. Even more serious was the erosion of the market. Living and working patterns changed over a couple of decades. Many of the housewives who had been at home during the day found jobs and careers. They bought cosmetics elsewhere, and they weren't at home when the Avon lady came calling. So Avon, in an attempt to improve its cash-flow situation, went looking for a smaller company that showed a steady profit. It found Tiffany & Co., the jewelers. Avon tendered an offer to the stockholders, and it was accepted.

The tender will usually come in the form of a public announcement, offering to buy outstanding shares of stock in the desired company at a price considerably above the book value or current market value. (This number is the value of a share in cash if all the liabilities were paid off and the remaining assets were divided by the number of outstanding shares. It's mostly a theoretical value anyway, since the price of the stock is determined by the daily auction process.) The immediate effect is that the stock in the desired company rises dramatically in value, often to a level near the offering price. Rumors often will precede an actual tender, which will cause a flurry of action on that stock. Naturally, everybody wants to own stock that is almost guaranteed to increase in value within a few days. When the actual tender is made, the trading may be so intense that the exchange will suspend all activity for a few hours, even a day or more, to give investors in the marketplace time to assimilate the news and decide just what the implications are. When trading resumes, the stock may open much higher, or lower.

The directors of the company being acquired may support or oppose the attempt. They will customarily issue a letter of their position to the stockholders and may even take out an advertisement in *The Wall Street Journal* and in prominent local newspapers around the country. At this point, the most propitious event for stockholders in the desired company is the arrival on the scene of a third company also interested in acquisition. This could signal the onset of a bidding war in which holders of that stock are almost sure winners.

As you choose stocks for potential investments, you'll want to watch for those companies that are most likely to be involved in some sort of merger. The best indication is a high ratio of assets to liabilities. Two-to-one is normal; a company with a ratio of 4-to-1 is a good candidate to be taken over because of its unusually fine cash base. Such a company, however, could also be involved in a takeover from the opposite side, such as a parent company. And that could have a far different effect on the value of its stock, as we'll see soon. I said earlier that the book value of a stock, usually somewhat meaningless, has little in common with the actual market price. But that is not the case during an acquisition, when the tendered offer is usually based on the book value, plus a premium. Savings and loan institutions, for example, are notorious for trading below book value. I was fortunate enough recently to have stock in a savings and loan that was selling at $8 a share, about 50 percent less than book value. But the stock nearly doubled in two days when an offer was announced.

If you are the owner of stock in a company that has been acquired, you will receive either cash for your stock in the amount specified by the offer, or an amount of stock in the parent company. You'll have the chance to vote on the offer, but your stock is subject to the decision of the majority of the stockholders in the company being acquired.

You can still participate to your own advantage in the merger even if you aren't fortunate enough to own stock in the acquired company. For instance, there usually is a time period of several months specified in a takeover offer. Because of that period of limbo, a stock usually will not climb immediately to the offering price. An offer of $33 per share in October, for instance, might push a stock up to just $28 per share in June. As the deadline approaches, the value of the stock is likely to climb, perhaps ¼ point or ½ point per week. One factor that limits the explosion of value of a stock that is being acquired at a premium is the possibility that the deal will fail to be approved by stockholders or by the proper government agencies. The rate at which the value of a stock climbs is usually a good indication of how a takeover or acquisition is proceeding. The floor traders are very aware of the recent developments in any major deal of this sort and their actions are usually a good barometer of the deal's chances of success or failure.

The situation can be much different if you happen to own stock in a parent company that is taking over a smaller concern. It's quite probable, in that case, that those shares will show an immediate decline in value. The money to pay for those acquired shares must come from either stock or cash profits. Such a major expenditure decreases the net earnings or retained earnings of a company, which makes the stock less attractive. This devaluation of the stock offers a possible opportunity for the would-be investor. You need to evaluate whether the acquisition will help the parent company in the long run. If that seems to be the case, then the stock, especially at its reduced price, may well represent an eventual bargain. Probably you won't be the only investor to notice the bargain. As others do, too, the price of the stock will rise. The key is to be among the first to recognize the good buy, to own the stock as the rest of the crowd begins to buy, and to ride with it toward the top of its run. That is the essence of investing in stock—flexibility and the ability to move in a timely manner on a recognizable trend.

You can get a good overview of the market by reading the stock quotations in the back pages of *The Wall Street Journal* every morning before the market opens. By keeping abreast of the market and scanning the quotations, you can have a good idea of what went on the day before, specific leaders, and specific losers, and you can try to spot patterns and correlate those patterns with any general or financial news that may have influenced the market. Often the first minutes of trading in the morning are simply a continuation of what was happening when the market closed the previous afternoon. It's like a horse race from the moment that the tape begins to move, and everyone is trying to bet on what stock is going to be the big winner of the day. (See the illustration on how to read a sample quotation in *The Wall Street Journal*.)

Sample Stock Quotation in *The Wall Street Journal*

(1) 52 weeks High Low		(2) Stock	(3) Div.	(4) % Yld.	(5) P.E. Ratio	(6) (100) Sales	(7) High	(8) Low	(9) Close	(10) Net Change
48⅝	19	Bally	.10	.4	16	649	27⅜	26⅝	26⅝	. . . . .

1. In the last 52 weeks, this stock has traded as high as $48⅝ per share and as low as $19 per share.
2. Name of company or stock.
3. Dollars paid per share per year.
4. The percentage return of the dividend in relation to the current price per share.
5. Represents the price of a share divided by earnings per share for a twelve-month period. In our illustration, Bally Mfg. is selling for 26⅝ per share and the stated P-E ratio is 16. If you divide 26⅝ by 16, the result is approximately $1.66, which represents earnings for the past 52 weeks.
6. Sales are reported in 100s, so multiply 649 × 100, which means 64,900 shares traded that day.
7. Stock traded as high as $27⅜ per share.
8. Stock traded as low as $26⅝ per share.
9. Stock closed at $26⅝ per share.
10. Stock closed at the same price as the day before.

This, I suppose, leads logically to the successful stock investor's most valuable attribute, the knack for spotting a trend. I mentioned in the first chapter—and I heartily believe—that women, especially homemakers, are in a fine position to discover what commercial goods are most popular, because they spend so much time in the consumer marketplace. That information can lead to some very profitable investments.

Therefore, in times of uncertainty and high inflation, when the economy seems to lack a specific direction, you could do much worse than to look to yourself and your friends for guidance. Ask yourself what people are doing, what they are buying, how they are spending money. This is logical because women are the traditional money managers for day-to-day purchases in the family home. They can spot trends in the appliance industry. They shop for Christmas toys. Every year there is at least one successful new toy that dominates the Christmas market; I'd bet that you could discover that winner by watching the reactions of your children and others in toy stores for a few hours. Probably they aren't much different from the millions of other children who will be asking for gifts during the holidays. If you pay attention to popular items, you'll probably become aware of aosing line as well. And as you'll see in a later section of this chapter, it's as easy to make money from a faltering stock as it is from a healthy one.

If you visit several stores looking for a particular product and find the supply low or nonexistent, you must decide whether you alone are seeking that product (which would imply that retailers aren't stocking it simply because it's so unpopular) or the shortage is caused by a widespread demand. Look for advertising campaigns. Conversations with store managers and with other shoppers can help you decide whether the shortage truly is a case of demand's outstripping supply. Retailers can tell you whether the shortage has been artificially induced by poor manufacturing and distribution methods.

Next you'll need to discover which company manufactures the product. Perhaps, in the case of the Christmas toys, you discover that your children seem to prefer three or four different toys all made by the same company, an even better indication that the company is putting out products that people want to buy.

At this point, a trip to your public library is in order. Most libraries keep in their reference shelves current copies of Standard and Poor's (S&P) index of stocks or the Value Line Survey. If the company is an individual business it will have its own proper heading. If there is no listing under the correct business name, you can assume that the company is a subsidiary of another. Standard and Poor's Corporate Records has a cross-indexing system that will help you discover what company that is. Value Line or S&P will contain a great deal of valuable information: at least a ten-year history of the company, the highs and lows of the stock over the years, vital statistics of the balance sheet, assets and liabilities, the officers of the corporation, current products in the company's line, and products projected for the future.

This listing also will contain an address of the company offices, from which you should request the latest annual and interim reports. You might want to follow up with more conversations with retailers and shoppers. Do all this as quickly as possible. You want to spot and anticipate trends, not follow them. As you do all this, keep in mind the relative size of the company (you can determine that by comparing its listing in S&P and Value Line with those of its main competitors). If the company is a large one, with a wide range of products, then the success of a single item probably won't have a drastic effect on overall earnings. If the company is small, then a single successful product will have a far greater effect on its earnings, and hence on the value of its stock.

An example is MCA, a virtually anonymous company to the average person when it released the movie "Jaws" a few summers ago. The movie became a phenomenon. The lines outside the theaters made news and so did the panic at the beaches that the movie created. That single successful film was enough to double the price of MCA stock within a few weeks. A year later, Twentieth Century experienced the same sort of bonanza with "Star Wars." Stock in the company nearly tripled. These opportunities were available to anyone who took the trouble to find out who had released these movies, and who was willing to gamble that the pictures would become the outstanding money-makers that they turned out to be.

That uncertainty, that chance of making such substantial profits in a short period of time, explains some of the continuing popularity of the market. My experience as an investment counselor has convinced me that a great many investors are seeking not only growth and income from their money, but also excitement. People are by nature emotional and action-oriented. The lure of the quick profit appeals to the greed that is, to some extent, within all of us. The market is a place where all your fantasies and fears can be played out.

I'm sure there isn't a single investor in the market who hasn't at least once scanned the list of stocks on the exchanges and wondered which one will be the next to skyrocket. That hunger, coupled with an understandable desire to hitch up to an upward-moving stock, produces an atmosphere perfect for the creation of suddenly vogueish, glamor stocks that can rise well beyond what the earnings of the company alone would justify.

In recent years, the perfect example was stocks in companies with gambling interests. Casinos make money; the earnings of Las Vegas casinos have proved that. Gambling and entertainment businesses also traditionally do well in rough economic times. This, combined with the legalization of gambling in Atlantic City, New Jersey, produced the ideal conditions for an explosion of the price of a gambling stock.

The explosion occurred when Resorts International, a company that specialized in resort and tourist facilities, announced that it planned to open a major gambling casino in Atlantic City. The company issued two classes of stock: Class A, with which shareholders did not have the voting privilege to participate in management decisions, and Class B, which gave stockholders voting privileges. Class B stock was the more attractive and it took off. In 1978 alone, the stock traded as low as $21 per share and as high as $321 per share. Subsequently it underwent a 3-to-1 split. Each share multiplied into three.

As this is written, in the summer of 1980, the stock is trading well below its high. Resorts International, as a leader in the penetration of a new market, got heavy play early from investors. Now it seems that the market is looking at similar companies that may have caught up with the early leaders in the field. A lot of the glamor has gone out of that particular stock, and many people would say that it is now trading at a more realistic level.

I'd like to mention a sidelight that I think illustrates the point that you don't have to be right in there with the big early leaders in order to make money from a trend. You can do this by examining the market, looking at some of the peripheral companies that may profit from a boom. You'll notice, for example, that many of the slot machines in casinos are made by a single company, Bally Manufacturing. That name might also be familiar if you've got teenage children who seem to spend half their time and all their allowances feeding quarters into pinball machines. Bally happens to make some of the most popular pinballs, too, and pinball arcades are very much in vogue right now. It should be no surprise that Bally became a very strong stock with that kind of impetus.

At the same time, you need to be aware of the pitfalls of investing in stock that rises by riding the coattails of another successful company in its area or by being a part of a trend. The semiconductor field faltered after 1974 when companies were caught with huge inventories after wage and price controls were lifted, but in the last couple of years they have enjoyed a booming comeback. The companies in that business are doing well across the board, simply because they are in a high-demand area, and investors are optimistic about any company manufacturing miniaturized electronic components. Unfortunately, not all those companies have the sales and management background to perform up to the price of the stock. In some cases, speculators and the uninformed public have driven up the price by buying great quantities of inexpensive stock in companies that are bound to suffer reverses. The result is that many bargain-hunters will end up holding junk, because even the momentum of the market cannot forever sustain an overly high price on stock in an inferior company.

In the semiconductor field, specifically, companies slumped because they found themselves in price wars. The public can now buy $5 and $10 pocket calculators, something that was thought impossible a few years ago. So even if the number of units sold has remained constant or has risen, the sales in dollars have slumped dramatically. I know of one electronics company that saw a drop in sales from $28 million to $2 million within one year. Almost always, my advice to investors is to seek out high-quality stocks that will stand the test of time, whatever the field.

COMMON AND PREFERRED STOCK

Many major companies offer two kinds of stock, common and preferred, each with its own advantages and characteristics. Both signify ownership in a corporation, with the rights to attend and participate in stockholder meetings and receive regular financial reports. Both carry with them the expectation of higher stock prices, but they pay dividends in different ways.

Common stock has no assurance of dividends, while preferred stock is sold with the guarantee that a dividend in a fixed amount will be paid as long as the company is solvent. Dividends on common stock, by contrast, are declared at the whim of management. They may not be issued at all, and if they are issued they can be in whatever amount management deems appropriate. Preferred stock's guaranteed dividend can be cumulative; if the company is unable to pay a dividend for a certain period, it must make up all such lost dividends before paying any other dividends. Preferred stockholders also have some advantages if the company goes bankrupt, a situation I'll discuss later in this chapter.

All this helps to make preferred stock more stable and less subject to severe swings in its value than most common stock. Preferred stock is often the choice of those who are looking for a predictable income from their stock investment, though the growth potential is far greater with common stock. Preferred stock is the conservative choice, and it fits investors seeking stability. But by hedging against the deep depression that the corresponding common stock might experience, the preferred shareholder also is taken out of the running for any soaring highs that the stock might experience. If a company does very well, in fact, the dividend paid to common shareholders might be higher than that fixed for the preferred stock.

One way of getting some flexibility in a preferred stock is to buy convertible preferred, which carries with it the option of converting preferred shares into a predetermined number of common shares. Once a company's common shares increase to a price above that of the conversion price, an investor might convert and liquidate if that seems profitable.

BONDS

Most of the debt of corporations today is from the issue of straight subordinated bonds. These are issued on the good credit of the corporation. Both corporations and municipal entities that issue bonds are rated by Standard and Poor's or Moody's, from AAA (the best) on down. But you can get a good idea of the creditworthiness of a corporation by comparing the interest offered on its bonds to those issued by others. The less reliable the company (or city), the higher the interest it will have to pay in order to attract buyers for the bonds.

A bond is basically an interest-only loan. When a corporation wishes to raise a large amount of money for a specific purpose, it issues bonds and offers them for sale at a given interest rate. When you buy the bond, you are lending money in the amount of that bond for a fixed period of time. During that time, you (or the party to whom you might sell the bond) will receive interest on the face value. Just as a loan comes due within a certain period of time, the bond can be redeemed after the date specified on the bond or be sold on the open market.

A bond differs from securities in that the bond doesn't represent ownership of the company (though some bonds, known as collateralized bonds, are secured by specific objects of tangible value, such as valuable equipment). Unlike stockholders, bond owners aren't privileged to participate in company decisions.

However, bonds are very much a marketable commodity. Their trading value can rise or decline as they are influenced by a couple of factors.

One of these is time. Some bonds are sold at a discount, below their face value. The situation is similar to that of the stock involved in an acquisition; as the bond gets closer to maturity, the value of the discounted bond may come closer and closer to its face value, depending on the company's financial condition.

But the main factors influencing the market value of bonds are the inflation and current interest rates compared to the interest rate paid on the bond. Suppose a bond were issued to pay 9.5 percent, when the current interest rate is 10 percent. If the interest rate rose, new bonds coming onto the market might pay 10.5 percent. That 9.5 percent bond would be less attractive, since a newer bond of comparable quality would be paying a significantly higher rate. Suppose, however, that the interest rates dipped to 8 percent. Good-quality bonds then would pay about 7.5 percent, and that 9.5 percent bond would sell at a premium, not at a discount. The rule of thumb is that as interest rates rise, bonds become less valuable on the market. The reverse is true as interest rates decline.

Convertible bonds are a type that can be converted to a certain number of shares of common stock at a predetermined price. Thus, the price of the convertible bond is tied into the price of the stock. Obviously the option of converting to common stock is worthless if the stock is selling on the market at a price well below that specified on the bond.

This is just one of the factors that you'll need to consider before deciding on a bond. Far more is involved than just the interest rate. A few years ago one of my clients invested heavily in bonds issued by a major United States-based airline. These were $1,000 convertible bonds paying 5.25 percent. Common stock in this airline had dropped to just two dollars per share, though, which made the convertible feature useless at the time. And with the rising inflation and interest rates, new bonds of similar quality were paying several percent more. These two factors had helped drive the price of the bonds down to $500 by the time my client bought the bonds. Subsequently, the interest rates rose even more and the bonds were discounted to just $160, for the airline had suffered several bad quarters and there was a genuine possibility that it would go bankrupt and would be unable to fulfill its obligation when the bonds came due in 1989. My client tracked me down at one of my youngster's soccer games. He was panicky, wondering whether he ought to sell at $160 and avoid a total loss.

We analyzed the situation. The airline company was one of the largest in the world. Its name was the source of a certain prestige abroad for the United States, and not long before, the United States government had helped Lockheed Corporation out of a tight spot with heavy loans. It seemed likely that such assistance might be forthcoming for the airline company if necessary. On the strength of that, I advised my client to hold the bonds that he already owned and to buy others at the discounted prices. In addition, I liked the looks of another bond issued by that same airline—collateralized bonds secured by the line's 747 passenger planes, valuable pieces of property that would more than cover the face value of the bonds if the company's assets were liquidated.

My client wasn't the only investor to take advantage of the bargain. A major financial publication ran an article pointing out the attractive price of these discounted bonds, noting some of the same points that I had made to my client earlier. Partly as a result of this increased interest, and partly because of more favorable financial reports in succeeding quarters, the company's stock climbed to over six dollars and the bond was soon selling at over $500 again.

It's indicative of the outlook of modern investors that the terms of recent bond issues have become shorter and shorter. Twenty or thirty years used to be common. Now terms of five years are not unusual. People simply are unwilling to have their money committed for a long period of time, especially in an era of rising inflation and interest rates, when the market for bonds is weak.

A last observation on corporate bonds: You should check to

see whether the bonds can be called at the discretion of the issuer. A bond that is callable is one that the issuing corporation may redeem under specified conditions before the final maturity date. If the interest rates drop, the company will very likely wish to pay off those bonds and issue others at a lower interest rate, and you will lose the advantage you've gained, since the bond will be paid off at the face value, not at the market value, which would be higher than the face value because of the higher stated interest rate on the coupon.

Municipal bonds have tax-favored status. They can be issued by a state, a city, or a municipal entity such as a water commission or a transportation authority. The interest from these bonds is exempt from federal taxes. If the bonds are issued by an entity in the state where you are a resident, the interest is also exempt from state taxes.

For corporate bonds, you'll want to know as much as you can about the company and its ability to pay the interest and repay the long-term obligation. It's also important—especially in the case of a marginal company—to know how many other bond issues the company has outstanding. If there are several, and they are due to mature before your own, you might be in a bad position to recover your investment if the company should fail.

One advantage of corporate bonds is that such information is readily available. You may have more trouble finding out what you need to know about the sometimes obscure governmental authorities that issue municipal bonds. Their balance sheets can be difficult to interpret. It sometimes seems that even the politicians who manage them don't truly understand them.

But I don't want to disparage municipal bonds. One of my favorite municipal bonds is one issued by the Bay Area Rapid Transit (BART) Authority, which operates a commuter rail system in the San Francisco area. BART trains have been plagued with technical problems, and the system hasn't lived up to expectations, yet I consider the bonds among the safest because they are guaranteed by the real estate taxes of Alameda, Contra Costa, and San Francisco counties. I recommend that my clients never buy municipal bonds below the "A"-level rating on Moody's or Standard and Poor's charts if they are looking for income. Bonds lower than that are discount bonds, selling well below the face value, and ought to be considered simply as speculation.

I feel that municipal bonds, because they pay a somewhat lower interest rate than corporate bonds, are most valuable to those in higher tax brackets—40 percent and higher. Say that newer municipal bonds are paying about 7 percent, and the rate for corporate bonds is about 9.5 percent (as was true in the summer of 1979). To bring you an after-tax yield of 7 percent in the 50 percent bracket, a corporate bond would have to pay a fabulous—and unobtainable—14 percent. But in the 30 percent bracket, that 7 percent can be obtained from a 10 percent corporate bond. In a 20 percent bracket, the yield from a 10 percent bond is a true 8 percent, which makes even a tax-free 7 percent a bad deal. To get true advantage from a tax-free bond, you need a heavy tax obligation in the first place.

OPTIONS

The listed-option market was conceived in the early 1970s, in Chicago, using as its basis approximately twenty-five stocks from a substantial high-quality corporation with a good earnings history and a large number of stockholders. The concept was to let speculators purchase, for just a few hundred dollars, an option that would allow them to buy one of those stocks for a specific price within a specific period of time. The number of stocks available in the option market is greater now, but the idea is the same: to give the adventurous speculator the possibility for a maximum involvement in the market, with the potential of a high profit from a minimum investment. Only the commodities market offers a greater potential for profit with a minimum investment in every transaction.

Since it seems that unfamiliar jargon is one of the stumbling blocks that first-time investors often confront, let me dispense with a few essential items of vocabulary first.

A *call* is an option that guarantees the buyer the right to purchase a specific stock at a specific price within a given time. (The maximum time allowed by the exchanges is nine months.)

The *exercise price* is the predetermined price at which the owner of the option may buy the stock. It is also known as the *strike price*.

To *exercise* the option is to actually use the right to buy the stock at the strike price. (Note, however, that you may not need to exercise the option to make money. The option itself can have a marketable value.)

If you should exercise the option, you will be buying stock that has been put up as collateral with a brokerage house. The owner of that stock, who sold the option, has had his or her stock *called away*.

A *put* is the right to sell a stock for a certain price within a certain period of time. Puts, like options, can be sold without any actual exchange of stock. To buy a put is to buy the right to sell a certain stock at a certain price within a given period of time. A put buyer is pessimistic about the future of the market for that stock and is hoping for a decline in the value of that stock.

A specific example may help make all this more understandable. I'll use a real stock, Eastman-Kodak, at hypothetical but plausible price levels.

Calls are sold for lots of 100 shares. We'll say that you have bought an option with a nine-month term at an exercise price of $90 per share. This option costs $400, or $4 per share. Therefore, the stock must reach $94 per share within the term of the option before you can exercise the option and simply break even. You could just as easily have bought or sold a put on those 100 shares of Eastman-Kodak.

Suppose, however, you have bought a call on Eastman-Kodak. You're hoping that the stock itself will rise quickly. If that happens, the value of the call would rise as well. If the stock should rise to $95 per share, the call would have a tangible value of $500, for it would enable you to buy 100 shares of stock, valued at $95 per share, for the price of $90 a share, or $9,000. But if a significant amount of time remains on the call, then it's likely to trade for even more than that, perhaps $900.

However, if the stock should decline from that $90 price, the call would begin to lose its value. If the stock should stay below $90 per share, there would be no point in exercising the option. And as time eats away at the brief life of the call, its value drops to almost nothing. Thus, the initial investment of $400 should be considered a total risk.

It wasn't just by chance that I chose a stock like Eastman-Kodak for this example. Kodak is solid, yet volatile. To imagine Kodak climbing 6 or 7 points in a week is not at all far-fetched. That volatility is essential. Slower-moving stocks aren't nearly as desirable for option buying because they don't stand the same chance of shooting upward quickly. An option on Kodak will still have some value with a month or two remaining, even if it should be a few points below the strike price, simply because that is just the sort of stock that could gain 10 points or more before the option expires. The same can't be said of some other corporations.

If you're lucky enough to own an option on a stock that rises above the strike price, then you face a quandary. Do you sell the option, or exercise the option and then sell the stock which you've bought in order to recover your profit, or exercise the option and keep the stock? Commissions and premiums play a part in the decision. I'll continue with this hypothetical example to show you how it would break down in one case. You can apply the process to any situation.

Let's say the Eastman-Kodak stock has risen to 95 points. Since the stock is well above the exercise price and some time remains on the term of the option, the call itself is valued at $900 on the option market. To simply sell the option would give a profit of more than $400, even after commissions, a profit of more than 100 percent.

Exercising the option means paying a commission to the broker, approximately $81 in the $9,000 transaction (100 shares at $90, the exercise price). You could hold the stock if you felt it seemed likely to become more valuable, but to do so would tie up the $9,000 that must be delivered to the broker once the purchase is made. If your original intention was to hold the stock, it would have been cheaper to buy the stock at $88 instead of buying the option at an exercise price of $90.

So most investors choosing to exercise the option at this point would immediately sell the stock to realize the profit. This, though, means another $81 commission. So the gross realized from the sale is $9,419 ($9,500 less $81 commission). The actual cost of the stock is $9,081 ($9,000 plus $81 commission). The net profit is $338, $62 less than the net profit from the simple sale of the option. Moreover, that $338 actually represents a loss, for the option that made the purchase of the stock possible cost $400 in the first place.

The decision to exercise the option becomes less clear-cut if the stock should rise higher above the exercise price, but you can't count on that happening very often. Most investors would be pleased with a 100 percent profit over a few weeks. To count on making money in the option market, you'd best be prepared to trade options, not exercise them. But you should know that this is an active market and the options must be closely watched. And you must be ready to take a loss when necessary. It's usually not a good idea to hold an option to the bitter end and take a total loss. By getting out earlier, you can recoup part of your original investment and put it to some better use. However, this means admitting to yourself that you've made a mistake and picked a loser. That's something most people find hard to do, especially early in their investing careers.

A somewhat discouraging word: Latest information as of

this writing is that 80 percent of those buying calls lose money. That's partly a reflection on the market. If you don't care to buck those odds, there's an alternative. You can sell calls, too, though to do so you should first own stock in a company on which options are traded (if you don't, it's called being naked).

You would deposit the stock with your broker with instructions to sell a call on it if possible. Again, we'll use the hypothetical example with 100 shares of Eastman-Kodak stock, this time looking at it from the perspective of the call-seller. The stock, remember, is trading at $88 on the market. The caller-seller offers the option at an exercise price of $90, saying, in effect, "I'll be glad to sell this $88 stock to someone for $90." You, the call-seller, would receive the premium of $400 as soon as the call was bought.

At this point, however, you have relinquished for the term of the option your right to deal the stock. It is in limbo, on deposit with your broker, while the call-buyer (or the person to whom the call-buyer might trade the option) decides whether to buy or not. When you've put the stock on deposit, you should be prepared to lose it; options are sometimes exercised. And be prepared, too, for the tax consequences. If you bought those 100 shares of Kodak at $20, you'd find yourself facing a hefty capital gains tax on the $7,000 profit. Counting the $400 premium from the original sale of the call, your total gain would be $7,400—which would be taxed as a long-term capital gain. (If the stock is not called, then the $400 premium alone is counted as a short-term gain.)

A put is somewhat similar. To continue with the above example, you might buy from another investor the right to sell those 100 shares of Kodak at $90 per share within a certain period of time. The put would cost $200 (the difference between 100 shares at $88 a share and 100 at $90) plus a certain premium that varies with the recent performance of the stock and the amount of time left in the put cycle.

As owner of this put, you'd be hoping for the price of the stock to drop. If the stock should drop to $80 per share, the true value of the put would be $1,000, the difference between the exercise price on the put ($90 per share) and the market value of the stock ($80 per share) multiplied over 100 shares. The put could be sold to anyone ready to sell 100 shares of Eastman-Kodak. The loss would be sustained by the original seller of the put.

The permutations are almost endless and are beyond the scope of this book. The Chicago Board of Options and various brokerage firms have detailed pamphlets to explain the strategies that are available. But the possibilities are so complicated and so involved that the individual investor is advised to start small and watch the market carefully.

SELLING SHORT

There are those who feel it's unpatriotic to sell a stock when it declines or to hope for it to decline. Thousands of smart investors, though, do that every month. The practice of selling short—betting on a stock's decline—is one way of coping with a slumping market.

To short a stock is, in practice, to borrow securities from their owner and deliver them to someone else. It's all very legal and acceptable.

Let's continue with our beleaguered Eastman-Kodak stock trading at $88 per share on the market. You, as an investor, feel that the stock will decline in value. You don't own any stock and don't want to own any, but you would like to profit from this analysis you've made. You order your broker to sell short 100 shares of Kodak. The broker then must check the brokerage firm's inventory of collateralized stock to see whether this is possible. (This is stock being held as collateral in a margin transaction. We'll discuss margin buying later; suffice it to say now that the brokerage firm has lent up to 50 percent of the cost of the stock and is now holding the shares as security until the loan is repaid.) If you've chosen a popular, widely held stock, you'll have no trouble finding shares to short. Kodak would be ideal.

If the broker gives permission to short the stock, that order would go to the floor. The specialist there on the floor of the exchange would, by a regulation called the Uptick Rule, wait until the first upturn in the price of the stock before executing the order. This is for the protection of the stock, so that investors cannot automatically force down the price of a falling stock. In this example, we'll assume that the stock, which traded for 88 when the short order was placed, climbs to 88¼ points. This upturn, or uptick, allows the specialist to sell 100 shares of Kodak for $8,825. Remember that these shares have only been borrowed; they must be returned to the brokerage firm's inventory.

Now you're hoping that the stock dives, the more quickly the better. We'll suppose that it does just that and drops to $73. At this point you instruct your broker to buy back the 100 shares. Now, however, they're selling for $15.25 less than when you sold them. The shares are returned to the inventory and you show a profit of $1,525, minus commissions.

If you're wrong, however, and the stock begins to climb, you stand to lose money in quantities that can be almost infinite if you don't set a limit. Remember that as the stock climbs you've got to make up the difference between 88¼ points and whatever level it may reach when you buy out of the deal. If you set an upper limit of 95, you must make up a difference of 6¾ points per share (95 minus 88¼) or $675. The only deadline on shorting is that imposed by your own financial abilities to deal with a loss. The exception is when you've shorted a stock that is not very popular. The brokerage firm could be forced to ask for the stock you've borrowed. You would be required to replace it at whatever the going price might be.

Shorting, needless to say, can be very rewarding, and very risky. But it ought to be obvious by now that you can't have rewards without at least an equal portion of risk.

MARGIN BUYING

Buying a stock on margin is another way of increasing the amount of stock that you can buy for a given amount of capital. It's done with a loan from a brokerage house, which puts up 50 percent of the price of the stock you buy. It's also possible to buy commodities contracts on margin, too. The margin percentage of commodities contracts can be much higher, since they tend to be so fast-moving.

The NYSE requires a minimum investment of $2,000 for margin buying of securities. If you bought 100 shares of $30 stock, you would still be required to put up $2,000 of the $3,000 price. The brokerage house could advance you only $1,000. If your stock order were $4,000, however, the house could then match your $2,000. For figures above $4,000, the 50 percent maximum applies.

A margin account is very easy to obtain, and it's done routinely. (By contrast, you'll discover that bank loans secured by stocks involve a tremendous amount of paperwork.) Brokerage houses are happy to extend a margin loan, for several reasons. First, it increases the volume of their business. Second, they often make a profit on the interest they charge. (Margin interest tends to be somewhat higher than that of a similar bank loan.) Third, the loan is secured by the stock itself, which the house retains in its inventory. The broker is protected by the "25 percent equity rule," a New York Stock Exchange rule that requires the house to sell off the stock if its price should drop to half the price at which it was purchased. (Most firms have requirements that are slightly stricter than that.) Suppose, for example, that you've purchased 100 shares of stock at $100 per share. You pay $5,000 toward the purchase; the brokerage house advances the other $5,000 needed. If the stock declines to $75 per share, the value is just $7,500, and your equity in the stock is just $2,500, or 25 percent of the original value. So the 25 percent equity rule is invoked and the firm sells the stock to recoup its investment. Your broker will try to notify you if the stock begins to decline to that level, but even if he or she is unable to contact you, the house still has the right to sell out the stock or request additional stock or cash once you've reached your 25 percent equity.

ODD LOTS

Any stock order of fewer than 100 shares is considered an "odd lot," in broker's parlance. This is worth mentioning for two reasons.

One is that odd-lot buyers are sometimes at a slight financial disadvantage. They pay a higher commission and are subject to a ⅛ point differential on the floor between the price at which the stock is being traded and the price at which the odd lot is actually purchased.

The other is that odd lots are the subject of a special Wall Street index. This is an indication of what the proverbial "little guy" sees in the market, and it is a Wall Street tradition to go in the opposite direction of the odd-lot index. If there are more buyers than sellers in odd-lot securities, the feeling is that the market will decline. The truth is that the "little guy" has been notoriously ill-informed about the doings of the market. Don't despair, however; you aren't doomed to failure simply because you are unable to afford thousand-share lots. Investors have made handsome profits in purchasing shares that are in odd-lot numbers. But do be aware that you may need a substantial rise in market value to achieve a reasonable profit due to a possible odd-lot differential and/or higher commission percentage. One method of avoiding extremely high commission percentages and those odd-lot differentials is to consider the purchase of a mutual fund.

MUTUAL FUNDS

Large-scale investors in the stock market don't entrust all their investment capital to just a few securities. They diversify, carefully selecting stock in companies that have a wide range of products and services. This provides a certain amount of protection against an across-the-board slump in the portfolio. Even if auto companies should lose ground because of an oil crunch, as they did in the summer and fall of 1979 and 1980, the increased profits of oil companies and airlines, with a corresponding rise in their stock prices, would help take up the slack.

The small investor hasn't the capital to buy stock in several different companies. Mutual funds, however, do provide the opportunity for profitable diversification, if they are carefully chosen and closely watched. Many allow investments as low as $100 for your initial transaction.

A mutual fund is a pooled investment in a large number of companies and stocks, a conglomerate that owns stocks in as many as 100 different corporations. Shares of some mutual funds are traded on the market. You can find daily quotations in *The Wall Street Journal*. Some specialize in a specific industry; others are more general. Some are oriented toward income, others toward growth. Some invest only in common shares, while others buy a combination of common and preferred. To choose the right one for yourself, you need a clear financial plan. You can then choose the one that best suits your objectives.

There are two specific types of mutual funds. An open-ended fund has an infinite number of shares; the more money that is put into the fund, the more shares are created. Closed-end funds have a limited number of shares that are traded on the market, the price being determined by supply and demand. Open-ended shares are traded at a price determined by the net asset value of the fund. Thus, the price is a direct reflection of the peformance of that fund and the performance of the different stocks within that fund.

In addition, mutual funds can be distinguished as "load" or "no-load" funds. A loaded fund is one in which a commission is charged on the purchase, the amount of the commission varying with the money invested: about 8.5 percent for the first $10,000, perhaps 7.5 percent for the next $10,000. (Be wary of brokers who urge you to take one large sum and divide it among two, three, or more different funds. That's a highly unethical way of making a larger commission. A broker makes more money from three 8.5 percent commissions on $10,000 than from a 6.5 percent commission for a single $30,000 transaction.)

Obviously, if you buy into a loaded fund, you should plan to keep your money invested for a fairly long term. The commission charged on each transaction discourages investors from hopping from one fund to the next. That's why I urge my clients who wish to invest in mutual funds to do so in funds that actually contain a family of different portfolios, each with a different objective. If you should decide that you'd like to move your money from a growth-oriented fund to an income-producing fund, you could do so without paying additional commission. Probably you would imagine that a no-load fund would be most advantageous. But such funds almost always charge management fees instead of commissions.

In choosing a mutual fund, you'll want to consult the Weisenberger Report, which gives past and current performances of all mutual funds and is available at brokerage firms and most libraries. Keep in mind that it is traditionally believed in investment circles that the top-performing fund of the year rarely repeats its performance the next year. The truth is that few mutual funds have performed reliably in the past few years. Most have failed to keep up with the rate of inflation. Money can be made in mutual funds, but such funds must be as closely watched as any other stock.

Mutual funds do have some advantages. Their diversification is one. Professional management and supervision may be another, depending on the expertise of the managers. Because of the nature of mutual fund transactions, any profit made from them is taxed as a long-term gain, which is another plus. You can request that your dividends be reinvested in the form of more shares. And because of the volume of business that mutual funds conduct, their investors avoid the crushing lows (but also the soaring highs) that other investors might experience in buying a single chunk of stock and waiting for something to happen.

Before choosing a mutual fund, you may wish to find out how the fund managers are compensated. I favor those funds that pay the manager a salary based upon performance every year. A manager whose group of stocks perpetually lags behind the general market should not be rewarded with a handsome salary.

You can obtain this information through your broker or through a simple phone call to the offices of the mutual fund in which you are interested. Most funds maintain a staff to answer public queries. I like to ask, as well, whether a fund manager is free to refuse some of the money that has been allotted to him or her to invest, to recommend that it be put elsewhere, without jeopardizing his or her own income. If a fund's analyst in the aerospace industry is pessimistic about the market in that area, for example, is he or she free to recommend that it be passed on to another area without reducing his or her own income? The analyst should be, in my opinion.

A fund that allows some internal flexibility and innovation is usually the best investment.

COMMODITIES

Commodities are all around us: cotton, potatoes, wheat, beef, pork, coffee, plywood, and lumber, among others. Because supply and demand are constantly fluctuating, there is money to be made and lost in speculating on what availability and demand will be several months in the future. Suppliers of these tangible goods offer to produce a given amount at a given price on a given date. Buyers offer to buy a given amount at a given price on a given date. When sellers and buyers agree on the terms, a contract is created, and those contracts are traded on the market. That seems straightforward enough, but the multitude of unpredictable factors that can influence supply and demand—weather, consumer tastes, and politics, as well as financial conditions—makes commodities a most volatile investment. Because of the margin regulations, it is possible to lose even more money than you originally invest. But there is also potential for huge profit. Commodities are a classic example of the maxim, "The higher the degree of risk, the greater the degree of return."

I like commodities because they allow the average person to take advantage of obvious shortages in the consumer market. To illustrate, I'd like to use a true story. I can't call the story typical, but it does show what commodities contracts are and how they can be used to advantage by someone who perceives an oncoming trend.

In 1976, I became a partner in commodities account with three friends. All four of us were involved in investment and financial planning, and we had seen how profitable a well-managed commodities account could be. We modeled our account on formal managed commodities accounts—a recent phenomenon—that use computers and careful monitoring of trends to guide investors. Many of these accounts had a guideline that if they lost 50 percent of its value, they would be terminated automatically. We decided to adopt that guideline and set up a $50,000 account. (Our initial investment, because of the margin requirements at the time, actually was much smaller. And we knew that because of the 50 percent rule we had adopted, we could not lose more than half our commitment on our first venture.)

We bought our first contract in late October 1976. We had noticed the price of coffee rising in the stores and had heard news of coffee trees becoming diseased in Brazil, so we made coffee our first purchase. We bought a contract of 37,500 pounds of coffee to be delivered in March 1977, paying $1.68 a pound, or $63,000. By February, when we decided to sell this contract, coffee was selling for $2.42 per pound on the commodities market. Our profit was 74 cents per pound on

37,500 pounds, or about $27,000. The coffee seller, remember, had promised to deliver coffee to us at the lower price. If coffee had dropped in price, we still would have been obligated to buy at the contract price. Thus, we'd have been forced to take a loss on the overpriced product.

Coffee, however, continued to climb. We still had not met our objectives, and we decided that coffee had not yet topped out, so we bought another contract at $2.21 per pound in January 1977. In two months, the price climbed to $3.23 per pound, which was near the top that it would reach. We decided to sell, convinced that the climb could not continue, that consumers would not pay continually higher prices, even for a staple such as coffee. Our profit from the second contract was $1.02 per pound, or $38,000.

We had made impressive profits by predicting that coffee would rise. Now we decided to act on our conviction that the price must soon plummet. In May, we sold short a coffee contract—the process is the same as shorting securities—and repurchased the contract at the end of June. We sold at $2.87 per pound and bought back at $2.46. The profit was $7,500 for a one-month transaction.

A look at the changing margin requirements for coffee contracts during this period shows just how a small investor can become involved in some heavy financial action if the timing is right. When my partners and I bought our first contract for coffee, the margin requirement was less than 10 percent of the value. The 37,500 pounds at $1.68 per pound cost $63,000. The four of us put up $5,000. By the time coffee reached the end of its run, the margin requirement for a 37,500-pound contract was $40,000. The change was for the protection of small investors, preventing them from losing more than they can afford.

Make no mistake: It is easy to lose a great deal of money in commodities. Let's look at exactly what might have happened if coffee had slumped badly instead of climbing when my partners and I bought that first contract.

Most contracts have a limit on how much they can drop in

value each day. The limit on this contract was four cents per pound per day. Our original investment was less than 10 percent of the purchase price. If coffee had dropped four cents a day, five days in a row—not an impossibility—our loss on paper would have been $7,500, more than the amount we first put forward. Often an individual speculator gets caught in a declining market, with the contract moving down at the limit each day. The only choice then is to wait for the market to settle down and hope that losses won't be excessive.

It's for that reason that I discourage "one-shot" ventures into the commodities market with just a minimal investment. Far preferable is the managed, or guided, account like those I mentioned earlier, on which our successful experiment was based. These accounts specify a minimum investment of at least $40,000, which provides a buffer in a down market and allows diversification into ten or fifteen different commodities. The pattern of commodities investing has been that the majority of trades—perhaps as many as four of every five— have been unprofitable. But those that are profitable tend to be very, very profitable. Diversification allows the investor to make up for the losses with a few large gains.

Commodities investing is not for the faint of heart. It is for those who can afford to risk, who are willing to accept some professional advice. This is one area where the average person is not equipped to properly evaluate all the subtleties of the market.

If you prefer to see what you can do yourself, read on.

HOW TO CHOOSE A STOCK

Over the years, I've become convinced that the average investor willing to do some homework can evaluate a specialized area of the stock market as well as 90 percent of the licensed brokers in the country. That conviction was only strengthened by my experience a few years ago when I taught a weekend crash course on the stock market to a group of career women and housewives, ranging in age from twenty-five to fifty, at the University of California, Santa Cruz.

A few days before the class met, *Business Week* magazine published an article dealing with the fast-food industry. On the first day of class, I lectured on the market and gave some simple rules for evaluating the information that is available to every investor considering a stock purchase. I showed the group how to determine book values, how to evaluate percentages, how to compare the market and book value increases, how to compare price-earning ratios. I chose seven fast-food stocks from the Value Line survey, and when the class adjourned that afternoon, I gave out an assignment that kept the students busy for several hours that night. I asked them to evaluate the stocks and to pick the one that seemed to have the best chance of increasing in value, using the standard that I had described.

The next morning the students returned with their choices. I discovered that almost all of them had been able to select the one stock that seemed most appealing, the stock of the Wendy's hamburger chain. The following months proved them right. Wendy's showed itself to be an aggressive and forward-looking company, and its stock climbed briskly. That was no surprise to the stock market neophytes who had met at UC-Santa Cruz that weekend, however.

What I taught those women was simple: I showed them what to look for in a stock, and I showed them how to apply common sense in evaluating a possible stock purchase. I've already shown how to look for trends as a consumer and how to use that knowledge in beginning your pursuit of a stock. But a beginning is all it is. It usually isn't sufficient that a stock be riding a wave; while such a stock may climb quickly, it is always the first to fall and it falls the hardest when vogueish investors lose interest.

Rather, once you've located a stock that is leading a trend, you need to determine whether that stock is capable of sustaining itself when the trend loses its glamor. To do so you must examine:

The balance sheet: Current assets should outnumber liabilities by at least 2 to 1. The greater the ratio in favor of assets, of course, the better. Available cash makes expansion possible. There are a few exceptions to the 2-to-1 rule. Chemical companies require a higher ratio because they expend so much effort in research and development, while railroads, utilities, and airlines often can operate successfully with less than a 2-to-1 ratio.

The earnings record: Earnings must have been consistent for the past several years. Peaks and valleys in an earnings record may appeal to the speculative investor, but that phenomenon is wrong for the first-timer on the market trying to select a solid stock selling at a bargain price.

The dividends record: Research dividends for at least the previous ten years. Dividends should have been paid consistently and should have increased over that period. However, don't give up on a stock that shows a single bad year out of ten. Check to see the cause of the problem. It's possible that a large nonrecurring capital expenditure during that year may have forced the company to cut dividends. Perhaps earnings have been plowed back into expansion.

The price-earnings ratio: You can compute the price-earnings ratio (P-E) by dividing the market price of the stock by the earnings per share, a figure to be found in most stock guides. For example, a stock selling at $30, with earnings of $6 per share, has a price-earnings ratio of 5 (30 divided by 6).

Lately, a P-E ratio of 10 has been considered optimal. A ratio a good deal higher or lower can be a sign of danger. A much higher ratio, for example, may indicate that investors have driven the price of a stock up beyond the level justified by the company's earnings, though a substantial increase in earnings can cause the same effect. A stock with a low P-E ratio may, indeed, be a stock selling at a price lower than it ought to, considering the company's earnings. More likely, though, the stock is priced low for a reason—inconsistency, poor management, or outside influences like government regulation that may affect the company's business.

When you have these numbers, you'll need to apply your common sense and your perception of trends. Look at the company's line of products in relationship to consumer tastes and preferences, bear in mind any other information you've collected from outside sources—newspapers or magazines, for example—and evaluate the management of the company if possible. Then project the company's earnings for a year or two in advance and predict as well as you can the amount of dividends, if any. Lastly, compare those figures with those from other companies in the same field. This ought to be the basis on which you select your purchase.

IF THE COMPANY GOES BANKRUPT

You should be notified by your broker if a company in which you've bought stock is in a precarious situation. If the company should fail and a receiver be appointed, you'll also receive notice. Often the notice will contain the credentials and prior expenses of the receiver.

There may be meetings of the affected stockholders. Discontented stockholders may band together and may even pool their resources for a class action suit against the managers of the company if they have evidence that mismanagement has caused the company's failure.

Three things can happen:

First, the company may fail completely. In this case, there is a high probability that all you will get from your investment is a tax loss write-off. There is a hierarchy through which liquidated assets of the company must pass. Taxes must be paid first. Then creditors must be totally satisfied. (These include bondholders.) Preferred stockholders are next entitled to whatever assets remain. Common stockholders are last on the list. Most often, they come out of the bankruptcy with only fancy wallpaper. The loss can be used to help offset taxes for the year.

Before this happens, however, the failing company may be acquired by a healthy firm. In this second instance stockholders may be offered cash or shares in the acquiring company in payment for their holdings.

Third, it's even possible that during the course of the bankruptcy reorganization, the new managers will turn the company around and make it solvent again. For that reason, make certain that a stock certificate is totally worthless, that the company is truly defunct and not just assumed to be by another corporation, before you discard old stock certificates.

SOURCES OF INFORMATION

To make intelligent decisions about possible investments, you need complete and accurate information. This is doubly true of the stock market. Luckily, there is a wealth of both general and specific data to guide you in your choice, and all of it is readily available.

Any broker can help you to locate annual reports, a prospectus for the stock you're considering, and any one of the several commercial stock guides. These are publications of a specific nature. You'll need to know what you're looking for before you spend much time with them.

A background of general knowledge is helpful in understanding the market and incipient trends, however. The daily newspaper can help. Weekly newsmagazines often are on top of important scientific, political, social, or economic news. Publications like *Forbes*, *Fortune*, and *Business Week*, to mention just a few, are good for news for and about business people. From them, you can read of important changes in management and the products of different companies. Often they offer analyses of stocks and different fields of business, and they comment on how political and legal news affects the economic sector.

But the one truly indispensable publication for anyone who is, or may be, an investor is *The Wall Street Journal*. For brokers, buyers, analysts, and speculators, the *Journal* is a part of the morning routine five times a week. The *Journal* is a fine newspaper, well respected by journalists around the country. It lacks only the latest scandals, murder, crossword puzzles, comics, and recipes that you'll find in your daily newspaper. Instead, it concentrates heavily on world and national news, especially that which affects the economy. And in the *Journal* you'll also find business news—news of mergers, acquisitions, changes in management, and coming products—that you won't get anywhere else. There are feature stories of general interest, and analyses of different sectors of the market. A rotating front-page column offers business analysis Monday and labor news Tuesday, followed by tax reports Wednesday, a business bulletin Thursday, and, on Friday, a somewhat gossipy business-political column that deals with matters outside the New York financial world. And every day, on the back pages, there is a complete and accurate listing of stocks from the previous day's trading on the NYSE and the American Exchange, in important over-the-counter stocks, and on the commodities, currency, and option markets.

PLACING AN ORDER

Once you've decided to buy a stock, bond, option, or commodity contract, the way to follow through is to place an order with your broker. So I think it's important for you to know something about dealing with brokers, about what happens to your order once you've placed it, about the kinds of orders that you can give, and about your rights in a relationship with a brokerage firm.

Actually, you'll need to have contacted a broker before you place your first order. You need not feel obligated to choose the first one you meet. You should feel comfortable with your broker's style and way of doing business, for if you become a serious investor, the two of you will be in touch often. You and your broker need to know and to trust one another. Do not, at any rate, simply call a brokerage firm and ask to speak to a broker. Your call will be transferred to an individual known as a "floor man." Since this is traditionally a low-priority position characterized by many aggravations and few rewards, it usually goes to a junior broker, perhaps one who has just received a broker's license. You want an experienced broker who understands the market. To find one, you might visit a brokerage house personally and explain specifically that you don't wish to deal with the floor man (or floor person), but someone who specializes in investors with objectives and needs similar to yours. Ask whether the house deals only with a minimum dollar account or is willing to work with an investor who is learning and may ask numerous questions.

Once you've met a broker and decided to work with this person, you should expect honesty and forthrightness in all your dealings. You ought to explain to the broker your position as an investor, including your objectives and the capital you have free for investment. This is the time to lay out the ground rules for your business relationship. If you expect a daily update of your investments, make that clear. (Be certain, however, that your account is such that it merits that kind of attention.) If you need research, make that understood as well. Whatever ground rules you may lay down, be certain that the broker knows that you expect to be informed of how your orders were executed, and at what price; of any threat to your collateral, if you are buying on margin; of any impending problems with companies in which you've invested; of any new factor that might affect the value of a stock the broker has recommended. Perhaps you don't wish to be called. You may initiate all contact, simply expecting good service on your orders.

There are numerous variations on the normal buy-sell order. These are some of them.

A *market order* is one that is executed at the current price at which a stock is trading when the order is placed on the floor. Note that although stock quotations usually are quite timely, there may be a discrepancy between the price your broker quotes and the price at which your order is executed. A market order can be either a buy or a sell order.

A *limit order* gives your broker numerical guidelines for a transaction. In the case of a limit buy order, you might give instructions to buy only when the price reaches a certain level. As an example, you might instruct your broker to sell a certain stock when it reaches 22 dollars, though it is trading currently at 25. When the stock hits the limit of 22, the order would automatically become a regular market order. Again, this limit can be applied to both buy and sell orders.

A refinement of this type of order is the *stop limit order*. In the example above, the broker would take 22 as a stop limit. That means that you would not accept a price below 22. There is a danger here: If the stock should fall to 21⅞ before the order can be executed, and if your broker is unable to contact you, he or she would be unable to execute the order. The stock could plummet to nothing without ever again climbing to the stop limit of 22. Still, limit and stop limit orders are helpful for those who want some control of their portfolio even if they are unable to make daily decisions.

There is a priority system on the exchange floor that could be significant to you if you ever should be involved with a hot stock that is quickly rising or falling. In that case, you will want your order executed as quickly as possible. The exchanges' priority system is a way of sorting out a pile-up of orders on a certain stock.

The most important distinction is time. Each order is logged in as it arrives on the floor. Whenever a conflict arises, the earlier order is executed first. If other orders are logged at the same time, then market orders are executed before limit orders. If all the orders are of the same type, then the next determination is size. An order of 200 shares would take precedence over an order of 100. There is one final determination. If two identical orders of the same size are logged at the same time, the final decision can be as simple and archaic as the flip of a coin.

It's quite possible that at some time you may have a disagreement with your broker about a specific transaction or about the general way your account has been handled. Into the first category might fall such disputes as a disagreement over the price you've paid for an order. You may discover that you've paid $33 per share for a stock that hit a high of only $32.50 on the date you made the purchase. Such disputes can be settled by following the order from the time it left the broker's office until the time the purchase was made and the price reported. This is possible because of the elaborate recordkeeping system practiced by the brokerage houses and exchanges.

Your complaint may not be so specific, however. You may be unhappy with the way you've been treated by the broker. Perhaps you feel that you've been pressured into making a great number of transactions (each one of which means a commission for the broker). Or you may believe that your broker has misled you with advice and has failed to give you an accurate account of the financial standing of the stock you decided to purchase.

Such complaints should be taken to the branch office manager. The record of activity in your account will be examined, and the broker will be given the chance to answer the complaints. You'll have a greater chance of having the matter settled in your favor if you have kept a record of all your conversations with the broker. You need to have documented support for your case.

And always, whatever the nature of your complaint, you stand the best chance of having any wrong corrected if you register your unhappiness early, the earlier the better.

THE STOCK MARKET AS AN INVESTMENT

There was a period, which ended about ten years ago, when an investor could hardly go wrong in the stock market. You could buy almost any security and expect to see it increase in value; the question was which would increase fastest. That was a golden time for the market and for the economy in general.

The onset of double-digit inflation and a prevailing political and economic uncertainty have changed that. It's now possible to lose a great deal of money in the stock market. Investments must be carefully considered and evaluated.

There are opportunities in the market nonetheless. For myself, I favor the commodities market over securities and options. Since I don't feel I'm sufficiently informed about all the intricacies of that market, however, I trust my investments to account managers who keep me informed of the status of my account. I have chosen not to trade on the stock market, thus avoiding any potential conflict with my clients' positions. The fact is that nobody can learn all there is to know about every phase of the stock market; the best that you can hope for is to survey all that is available, try several different investments on a limited basis, and finally settle on one that suits your tastes, temperament, and overall financial plan.

And lastly, when you've hit a winner, don't fall prey to the "big kill syndrome," which is just another form of greed. You should have an expectation, a goal, for every investment. Once you've reached that goal, don't stay around to milk more out of it. Conversely, don't stay too long with a stock that has begun to fall decisively. There *is* a limit to every rising stock; unfortunately, there is no limit on a falling one until you get down to zero.

8

INVESTMENTS (2): REAL ESTATE

It's understandable if a good deal of the material we've covered so far is difficult for many of you. After all, many of the concepts with which we've dealt, like commodities contracts, securities, and inflation, are abstract and intangible. That, perhaps, explains much of the popularity of real estate as an investment. Real estate is solid, visible, easily understood. Moreover, it has an intrinsic value that is as old as humanity itself—it is shelter, for either business or personal purposes.

That alone, however, does not account for the passion with which many investors have approached real estate recently. The popularity of real estate is well founded. As we saw in the chapter dealing with inflation, real estate has in the past decade proved to be one of the very best hedges against the deterioration of the dollar's purchasing power. Someone buying an average home in 1968 would have paid about $26,000. The same home in 1978 was valued at $58,000. A good deal of that increase can be attributed to inflation alone. But even after the dollar's diminishing buying power has been taken into account, the owner of that average home who disposed of the property after ten years still showed a profit of $4,500 in 1968 dollars, or nearly $10,000 in 1978 terms. There's another factor to be considered as well. A home isn't merely an investment; we expect more of it than appreciation. Since housing is going to be a perpetual expense in the budget for most of us, the money we pay to have a roof over our heads might as well be paid into a mortgage, from which it is returned to us once the house has been sold. Add to that the tax advantages inherent in mortgaging a home, and the lucky homebuyer of 1968 seems to have done very well indeed.

Banks and savings and loan institutions are recognizing the price of housing and the fact that a home is now a major investment. The rule of thumb used to be that banks discouraged homebuyers from paying out more than 25 percent of their monthly income for housing. In recent years, though, I have seen banks and savings and loans approve loans for which the monthly payments represented as much as 40 percent of a family's after-tax income. This is logical, for the money that is spent for a home isn't lost; most often, it is returned with a handsome profit when the property is sold.

It doesn't take much of a financial whiz to see that real estate is one of the more promising investments you can consider these days. That isn't always true; there are some times when other investments, like the stock market, offer even more growth potential than real estate. This is not such a time. The stock market, for one, has been a failure for many as a hedge against inflation. Real estate, on the other hand, has absorbed the punishment handed out by the shrinking dollar and has generally managed to increase in real value. In this chapter, I want to review the various ways that you may invest in real estate, either individually or with partners: in single-family homes, multiple dwellings, apartments, commercial complexes, and raw land. All offer various attractions. Each has its own danger areas and quirks with which you should be familiar. Despite the price increases of the past few years, it is possible to lose money in real estate by poor judgment, haste, or failure to consider adequately the consequences of the purchase.

I have a client who managed to lose money recently by buying a single-family home in a very affluent neighborhood. He and his family originally intended to live there and sell the home in which they had been living. But a combination of circumstances, including the fact that he suddenly realized he would be facing a daily commute of twenty-five minutes instead of just five, forced him to change his mind. Consequently, he and his family were making two mortgage payments. He rented the new home, though the rent he was able to get for the house fell $400 short of covering his new mortgage payment. (This was a very expensive home.) The house was over twenty years old, and my client within a year found himself paying for a new roof and repairs to the electrical and plumbing systems. The cost for repairs in the first year: $6,000.

One tenant cared for the place well, but a second abused the property, and the security deposit that the tenant had posted was hardly enough to pay for the repairs. That meant more time, more trouble, more money put into the house. (This is one of the problems landlords face. There are legal remedies, but often the remedies are as expensive as the original damage.)

After eighteen months of this, my client sold the home for $25,000 more than he paid for it. But that was not a clear profit. Once he had taken into account the unexpected repairs, the $8,000 commission paid the real estate agent, the negative cash flow of $400 every month for a year and a half, and time, energy, and the ever-present effects of inflation over eighteen months, my client found that he had actually lost money on the deal.

But that doesn't have to be your experience. Your venture into real estate can be far more profitable and pleasant if you follow a few simple guidelines.

SINGLE-FAMILY HOMES

Of course, this is the most common type of real estate purchase. Later in the chapter, I'll list some of the things you ought to do before purchasing different kinds of real estate, some of which can be applied to a single-family residence that you are buying for your own home. But I'll confine myself here to things you should look for when buying homes simply as an investment.

More and more people are buying homes to rent out, so that tenants can make the mortgage payments while the property appreciates. I have clients who own strings of ten or fifteen homes. They've turned this into such a business that the sideline became a full-time occupation, and they quit their former jobs.

So many people have taken this investment path that I feel it's not as potentially lucrative as it was just three or four years ago, when home prices really began to explode. I base my reservations on the belief that prices simply can't continue to rise as they have. In some areas, I feel, the rise of prices will slow down drastically.

Having said that, however, I think there still is a way to make good money in a short period of time. You'll simply have to be more careful and more selective than would have been necessary a few years ago. My advice is to look for areas that haven't yet experienced the boom that recently swept through California and other hot housing areas. Search for areas where major manufacturing and industrial firms may be relocating, places that seem on the brink of major growth; cities in the Pacific Northwest and the so-called Sun Belt of New Mexico, southern Colorado, and Texas seem likely. The general idea is to look for cities where the living is still somewhat cheaper than in big East Coast population centers, where city and county government is friendly to growth and new industry, where state laws—as in Nevada—give a tax break to relocating corporations. Consider areas that have energy resources. Those are the very elements that companies seek when they're looking for a place to locate a plant. Where there is a big plant, there will be jobs, and that will mean an influx of workers and a demand for housing.

There's another way of making quick money with a home. I'd look for the junker on the block, maybe the least attractive home in the immediate area, and see just how low the seller will go in accepting a bid. The idea is to get the price you will pay as far below the prevailing standard of the neighborhood as possible, then clean and paint and generally tidy up the place before immediately putting it back on the market. I'll discuss renovations later in the chapter, but that's not the sort of thing I'm talking about here. It's amazing what a fresh coat of paint, a few days' worth of cleaning, and $100 in garden plants will do for the value of a home. (Appraisers seem to love the orderliness and color that petunias will bring to a home. I've seen a few newly planted petunias make a difference of $5,000 in two appraisers' estimates of the value of a home that otherwise was exactly the same as it had been.)

Remember that your profits on such a sale will be taxed as short-term gains, unless you simultaneously buy another property at the same price or a greater price than the selling price on the first home. With personal property, you are allowed eighteen months to buy another home. There is no grace period at all with investment property.

That introduces an element that bears mentioning: United States income tax laws make a specific differentiation between personal property and property bought to produce income. With multiple-unit buildings such as duplexes, triplexes, or apartments, the portion in square footage that is used by a live-in owner is regarded as personal property, while the remaining percentage is treated as income property. It's possible to change the character of property from personal to income by renting the house for at least six months. This is the course I often suggest to widows or divorcées who own a home that is too large and too expensive for them, but that they can't sell immediately for sentimental reasons. I advise them to leave the house, rent or buy another, and rent their own to someone else for at least half a year. By that time their sentimental attachments usually are not as strong; they get all the tax advantages of owning income property, and then they can sell the house and trade up to a duplex or small apartment. When a property is traded or exchanged, the taxable gain is deferred.

The drawback to all this is that acting as a landlord isn't for everybody. It isn't profitable, for one thing, to attempt to keep your rental property the most charming house on the street. That isn't to say that it shouldn't be clean, neat, and safe, but your tenants probably won't be as careful of the house's appearance as you are, so you'll be fighting an expensive losing battle if you try to keep the place looking pristine. If it would seriously bother you to own property that isn't just right, then maybe being a landlord isn't for you.

Even tougher is the fact that renting a home, or a series of homes, is a business and has to be approached as such. That means that there are times when you'll have to do things that may come hard for you—like pestering tenants who have fallen behind on their rent and even evicting those who mistreat the property or are seriously in arrears with their rent. That's a task that some people just don't want to do.

There are a couple of alternatives. One is to get into another phase of real estate—renovating—which I'll discuss later in this chapter. The other is to hire a management firm that will, for a percentage of the rent, assume such duties as interviewing prospective tenants, collecting rent, arranging for routine and extraordinary maintenance (the cost of which the landlord will bear), keeping track of the house's condition and evicting any tenants who fail to live up to the terms of the rental agreement.

These management firms are available for all kinds of rental housing. Most specialize in one type or another, so do a little legwork before you decide which firm to hire. Call companies you see listed in the Yellow Pages until you can choose from several that specialize in the kind of housing in which you have invested. Compare their prices and services. Make sure that the company is experienced. Ask for references, and check the references you're given. That means calling the owners of other properties and maybe even driving to visit those properties, to see whether they are well maintained and clean.

You will save a good deal of money if you can manage the

place yourself. But it's money that you will *earn*. Managing just four or five homes can turn into a full-time job, especially if they are older homes. Remember, you as the landlord are responsible for the condition of the property. That means you must be handy at minor plumbing, electrical, and carpentry jobs. You must know when to give up and call an expert. And you have to be ready to come to the rescue at almost any time. Calls for help can come at any hour, any day.

Many of the same considerations apply to selling a house yourself. Undeniably, there is much money to be saved— $6,000 to $7,000 in commissions on the sale of a $100,000 house. Some people can do the job effectively; others aren't as suited to a task that includes being able to write an attractive advertisement for the newspapers and making available sufficient time, especially on evenings and weekends, to show the house and follow up on telephone inquiries from prospective buyers. You must know the current state of the money market in your area—who is lending how much money at what percentage rate—so that you can steer buyers toward the right lending institution. It means understanding the workings of title companies and escrow companies and banks, and understanding how to fill out contracts and deposit forms. Some people acting as their own agents get discouraged when the home they're selling doesn't move the first weekend it is offered on the market. That is understandable, for your time is probably more valuable than you think, and you can devote many dozens of hours to the job of selling before you are finally successful. I prefer to get the exposure of the Multiple Listing Service. Somebody else can earn that commission.

Probably some mention ought to be made of mobile homes here. The market is growing tremendously, and for good reason. Mobile homes provide a real alternative to buying a conventional home, with the advantages of home ownership. It's possible to buy some of the nicer mobile homes for under $40,000, with 10 percent down or even less. They are true homes, especially the deluxe double-wide types. In fact, architects and builders of new homes could learn a few lessons in space utilization from the designers of these mobile homes. There's little wasted area.

The parks designed for mobile homes have changed a great deal. They used to have an image as a haven for retired persons. Now, though, they are popular with newly married couples. The grounds have the amenities of a condominium complex, with swimming pool, recreation room, well-kept grounds, and a play area for children.

Most significant of all is the changing attitude of lending institutions, which have begun to recognize that mobile homes can appreciate in value and represent a solid investment. Consequently, they have relaxed their rules for financing mobile homes and have even begun to refinance them. It is this development, most of all, that makes mobile homes a realistic choice for those either seeking a first home or looking for a way to begin investing in real estate. (In many cities with tight housing, there is a sizable rental market for mobile homes.)

MULTI-UNIT HOMES

Into this category I put duplexes, triplexes, four-plexes, even six-plexes, anything between a single-family home and a typical apartment house. Though most of what I've said about single-family homes as rentals applies as well to these buildings, I've included them in a separate section because they offer the unique chance for a landlord to live in the building while collecting rent that may well cover the entire mortgage payment.

Generally, these buildings feature an owner's unit that is somewhat bigger and nicer than the others in the building. If you choose not to live in the building, that unit can be rented, and its features usually will fetch a somewhat higher rent than those of the other units. Should you decide to live on the premises, you'll find it necessary for tax purposes to compute the total square footage of the building and to find what percentage of the floor area the owner's apartment comprises.

APARTMENTS

Apartment buildings can range from large converted homes with six or eight private rooms to multibuilding complexes with hundreds of units. Not many investors will be able to start a career in real estate by purchasing a huge apartment complex. Most, in fact, should not start that way. But I will note that the greater the number of units, the greater the chances of the gross income's covering expenses and mortgage payments. The chances of having a negative cash flow increase with smaller buildings with relatively few units. Owners of such buildings often have to supplement the rental income with funds from some outside source. With larger apartment buildings and large commercial complexes, agents' fees and commissions become quite negotiable. At the other end of the scale, they tend to be firm and proportionately higher.

In whatever size, apartments are major investments that ought to be carefully considered. Later in this chapter, I'll discuss some of the factors that ought to be weighed in such a deal. Let it suffice to say now that you need professional help in such an undertaking. There are numerous pitfalls both in the buying and in the running of such buildings. Most cities and states, in fact, require an on-site manager for buildings with sixteen or more units.

COMMERCIAL COMPLEXES

Some of the developments represented here constitute the upper end of the real estate investment spectrum. Shopping malls and downtown office buildings are well beyond the reach of most of us, at least as single investors. But much of the thinking that goes into such projects can be applied to smaller ventures as well.

Walk into any modern shopping mall and you'll notice that the shopping center is dominated by two or three major stores—Safeway, perhaps, or Macy's, Sears, or Penney's. They are known as "anchor tenants" for the project. They serve a number of purposes.

Usually they are the first tenants committed to the mall, maybe even before construction begins. These companies sign long leases, providing security for the builders and the owners, and the leases probably provide stipulations that the rental is to increase automatically as taxes and utilities become more expensive.

Moreover, the major tenants attract the smaller stores that hope to take advantage of the heavy foot traffic that such big stores guarantee.

It's true that such deals are far beyond the reach of most of us. But it may be feasible for you, or you and a group of your friends in partnership (more on that in the next chapter), to put together a deal for a smaller commercial office or retail complex. You could design the project around a couple of anchor tenants. A medical lab might be one example. It would tend to attract other doctors and dentists, as well as a pharmacy.

Once more, however, let me reiterate the value of professional assistance. The financiers who put together huge shopping malls won't dream of doing so without specialized, experienced lawyers and accountants. There's no reason why you should be different.

RAW LAND

Raw land, in my opinion, is the riskiest form of real estate investment. It might even fall into the category of speculation, for there are a lot of things that can go wrong between the time you first decide to buy the property and the time you eventually want to dispose of it.

There have always been a lot of uncertainties connected with unimproved land: The market value often is difficult to determine; the land can be difficult to resell if you're trying to liquidate your investment; brokers' fees are a high 10 percent (nonnegotiable, in my experience). An even greater hazard has been introduced in the past several years with the advent of controlled-growth zoning laws and increasingly militant conservationist groups. That means that building permits often are difficult to obtain and that there is a growing chance that the land you buy will be affected by ecological laws or regulations.

Environmental groups are strong and well funded in many parts of the country. Before you buy raw land, make certain that you can obtain a permit for the kind of building that you want to put up. If it seems that you will face opposition on environmental grounds, ask yourself whether you have the time and the money to fight the legal battle and to comply with all the regulations that you'll be facing. I know of one developer who spent $250,000 to prove that a butterfly that was found in an area where he hoped to build wasn't actually unique to that one spot. Not many of us have the backing to afford that kind of effort. Even if you should eventually win your case, the appeals process can consume two or three years of your time. Your land, in the meantime, will be of little value to you or any other potential builder.

You can avoid those hassles by buying land that already is approved for development. That, however, will be considerably more expensive and may pose perils of its own. Be exceedingly careful of any planned development or tract that is offered for sale to the public.

In particular, I urge you to be wary of the sort of large developments that include hundreds or even thousands of small tracts in a single huge development. Often the entrepreneurs behind these deals hire a TV or screen personality to help promote the sales of the lots. They will extend an offer of a free plane ride to the property and a complimentary dinner on the site, as well as a tour of the development. Keep in mind before you accept that the salespeople at these developments are trained in high-pressure sales tactics and that you may be letting yourself in for some intense promotion. One of my clients and his wife once accepted such an offer. My client told me later that he found it virtually impossible to get back on the airplane for the return trip without signing an agreement to buy a lot.

Another common sales tactic is to display a map of the property dotted with colored pins that are supposed to denote lots that already have been sold. When you are taken on your tour, you may hear a voice coming from strategically placed loudspeakers, announcing every couple of minutes that different numbered lots have just been sold. It is more than just possible that the lots haven't really been sold and that the announcements are designed to create the impression that the land is selling out fast, with the implication that you too ought to get in on such a hot deal.

For this reason, many contracts with reputable sellers contain a clause that allows you a time period of up to thirty days to consider your purchase and then back out if you feel you've acted hastily. Don't be afraid to exercise that option if you have second thoughts. Better to admit that you've goofed now than later, when a mistake would be much more expensive and embarrassing.

RENOVATIONS

Renovation is a somewhat specialized real estate sideline that may appeal to those who get satisfaction from restoring an old building to its original glory and who may not have the mental attitude necessary to run a rental business efficiently.

A renovation project can take several forms: a fairly new building that has been abused; a single-family house that is now outmoded and needs updating in the kitchen and bath; a dilapidated old building that needs complete gutting and rebuilding. The size of a building isn't necessarily as important as the kind of work that is required. Buying new paint, carpets, and drapes for an entire apartment house might not be as expensive as completely redoing a single-family home from basement to roof.

There are special tax advantages to renovating and restoring buildings that have been found to have special historical significance. The owner is allowed to declare depreciation that may be far beyond the down payment on the building and the cost of the renovation. If the building is sold, you must then declare or recapture the excess depreciation. You may be able to get around that by refinancing the building to obtain dollars that aren't taxable.

EVALUATING A PROPERTY

Some of the criteria I will list here apply specifically to large rental complexes like apartment buildings and commercial buildings. But there are some basic standards that you ought to apply to every purchase, steps to help ensure that you're getting what you pay for in a piece of real estate.

Try to establish the value of the property you're about to buy as closely as you can. Compare the prices to the advertised prices of other similar properties in the same area. Hire a certified appraiser, if necessary, to inspect the property and judge its value.

Carefully examine the property and check its physical condition. If you are buying a single-family home, remember that the furnishings of the present owner will not be staying as part of the deal. Ask yourself how the house will look without the furniture, rugs, and pictures. Get in writing which of the appliances, if any, are to stay. When you are buying into a new development, don't take the word of the salespeople that sewers, water and gas lines, and paved roads will be constructed. Get it in writing as part of the contract, and if the developer is leery of making that legal commitment, then you ought to be leery of buying the lot.

If you are buying a house or a duplex or a triplex for rental income, find out what similar rental homes in the area are bringing each month. (The classified ads in a daily newspaper will provide a guide.) Determine whether the rental income you expect, minus normal expenses, will be enough to cover the mortgage payments.

If you are planning to invest in a major apartment complex, the process of evaluation is even more detailed. I have a long checklist that must be completed before I will commit myself or my partners to purchase.

At the very least, you should consider the following:

—What is happening in the rental housing market in that area, what is available, and what rents are being charged.

—What kinds of tenants the apartment is likely to attract, with special attention to probable income level. It's important that tenants be compatible. That means similar ages and social backgrounds. (You wouldn't want an apartment of two or three singles living next to a retired couple, for example.)

—The profile of the tenants already occupying the building: how well they have treated the building, how prompt they have been in paying their rent.

—The physical condition of the building and furnishings, if any. Plumbing and wiring are important, of course. You'll need to know whether there are any outstanding code violations that will have to be corrected. Replacing drapes and carpets can be expensive. I was once involved in a partnership that was forced to replace a substantial number of the refrigerators in a sixty-unit building.

—The nature and status of the community surrounding the building. Does it seem to be prosperous and growing? A failing neighborhood will tend to drag a building down with it. If you plan to rent to families with children, are schools nearby? The geographic location of the building can be important, too. A building near an ocean beach is subject to far more wear from the elements than an identical building inland.

—The rents being charged for the building, and how long they have stayed at that level. It would be difficult to raise rents immediately if they have recently been increased, though this dictum doesn't necessarily hold if the higher rent is accompanied by visible improvements to the property to make it cleaner, safer, more attractive.

—The gross multiplier of the area in which you are planning to buy. This figure is the ratio of the price of the building to the annual gross income it brings. It is fairly uniform in any given community, and it varies according to the affluence of the area and the demand and availability of rental housing.

For example, in the area where my office is located, Palo Alto, California, the gross multiplier ranges from 12 to 15. That is, the value of the building could be 12 to 15 times greater than the annual rental income. This is due to the value of the land, the limited housing available, and the general prosperity of the area. In a slum area, an apartment house identical to a house in Palo Alto might have a multiplier of no more than 2. You could, theoretically, pay off the price of the building with two years' rent. That doesn't mean that this property is a better deal, however. There are reasons why the price is so low compared to the income received. One of my clients who was involved in such a bargain property in an extremely depressed neighborhood once walked away from his holdings and left them to the city, rather than pay the huge heating bill and legal expenses incurred in dealing with a tenant group that generally cared very little about the condition of the property.

—The lot size and legal description. (This applies to any property you're thinking of buying.)

—Any rights-of-way or encroachments that might prevent you from adding on to the property or adding improvements like a laundry building or swimming pool.

—The availability of on-street parking if a parking lot is not included with the property.

—The possible maintenance costs of swimming pools, patios, gardens.

—The legal status and acceptability of condominiums, if you intend to convert the property.

—The condition of the elevator, if any. Is it up to code?

—The cost of utilities, if they are borne by the landlord.

—The age of the building, and the length of time since the last major renovations.

The National Institute of Real Estate Management has a guideline for expenses that a landlord should expect, expressed in percentages of the gross income. With few exceptions, it is a rule of thumb for property from a duplex to a major apartment house. The list includes 5 percent for management fees (which would not cover the expense of a live-in manager). The percentage will probably be higher for smaller properties. Other items are legal and accounting fees, 1 percent; real estate taxes, 10 to 20 percent, varying in some areas; 8 percent for gas and oil and electricity if the landlord pays utility bills, higher in some extreme-temperature areas; upkeep, painting, and gardening, 4 percent; overall maintenance, 5 percent; insurance, 2 percent; and wiring, roofing, and plumbing, 5 to 10 percent as an average over several years. Remember that these percentages may vary, though the total comes to 40 to 45 percent for ongoing expenses. The rest would go to debt service and the establishing of a reserve for large expenses.

DOWN PAYMENTS

You ought to know by now that I'm an advocate of using other people's money as much as possible, especially during highly inflationary times. But there are limits. You have to be sure that you are capable of making the payments on the mortgage.

Banks and savings and loan companies have their own formulas for determining how much debt they will allow a party to undertake. If you wanted to buy a house costing $100,000, you would be required to put down a minimum of 20 percent, or $20,000. To qualify for an $80,000 loan, you would need an income of at least $35,000 a year, even higher if you had other large debts or an unusual number of small debts. Should your annual income fall below that level, you would qualify for a loan only if you could put down additional money to reduce the size of the loan you would need. Failing that, you would need to have a cosigner whose credit is acceptable to the bank, who would be liable for the debt if you should fail to make the payments.

The down payment for raw land usually is 10 percent, with the remainder to be paid over a ten-year period on a private contract between buyer and seller.

Apartment buildings generally require a 20 percent down payment. Often, however, it is possible to work out a deal with the seller, who takes back a second trust deed for several years and thus reduces your own initial commitment. This leaves you some operating capital with which to improve the property, enabling you to raise the rents to help pay the cost of the mortgage and the second deed of trust. On apartments in which I've put together partnership investments, we've been able to reduce the down payment to as little as 15 percent in this way. The note matures in five years, at which time we plan to sell the property anyway. Thus, our only expense in servicing that debt is in paying the interest on the loan.

If you are planning to raise the rents after buying the property, you should write up a projection at least three years into the future showing what the increased revenues will mean over that time. This might help convince the bank officers or loan committee that you will be able to cover the mortgage.

Until recently it was universal practice when a house changed hands for the original mortgage to be paid off automatically and the buyer to take out a new mortgage at the current interest rates, which usually were higher than that of the old note. A recent California court case, *Wellenkamp vs. Bank of America*, allows buyers to assume the current mortgages on the homes they are purchasing and to use that credit to supplement the financing they must obtain. (A second mortgage must still be taken out to finance whatever portion of the sales price the down payment and the original mortgage do not cover.)

The way interest rates on mortgages have risen lately, this represents a big difference in monthly payments. The buyer may be assuming or "wrapping" (to use the jargon of the business) a mortgage as low as 7 percent, while interest rates for new loans may be 12 percent or higher.

As with any other major financial commitment, it's important to do some shopping and comparing when you're looking for a mortgage. You can do this by telephone. You should tell the loan officer the amount that you'll be wanting to finance, and whether the loan is for investment or personal property. (You may find that investment loans are more difficult to obtain.) Among the answers you want are the maximum amount the bank is usually willing to lend, the time period for processing a loan application, the loan fees or "points" currently being charged, the current interest rate, and the rules regarding prepayment penalties.

All these items can vary from one institution to another, and a couple of hours of research can repay themselves many times.

9

INVESTMENTS (3): LIMITED PARTNERSHIPS

PROBABLY you've been dismayed at the size of some of the numbers I've thrown out in the preceding chapters. If you're like most of us, you know that you'll never be able personally to finance the purchase of a $750,000 apartment house or the construction of a shopping center costing several million dollars. But that doesn't mean that you can't be a part of these money-making deals.

The truth is that very few people actually have the resources to do these things without help, and most of those few who do have the money choose not to. It is far more common for the developer of a project to take in several partners—or several hundred—to help finance the cost and to share in the profits. As a partner, you may invest no more than a few thousand dollars. The potential return from the right investment can be several times that amount, if you choose carefully and luck is on your side.

The partnership can take the form of a *joint venture,* in which several people pool their resources for a specific project. You could do this with several friends, putting up the money for the down payment on a house, taking out a loan, and letting the rental payments cover as much as possible of the mortgage cost of the house. In any joint venture, the partners all share the profits and liabilities, according to the percentage of the start-up money they advanced originally. The partners in the joint venture are responsible for decisions made by the group. Each is liable for part of the debt and is entitled to part of the profits.

In the example I mentioned, the partners in the house rental project all would be listed on the mortgage. Each would file a net worth statement and financial statement with the application for the loan. If the rental payment didn't cover the monthly mortgage payment, each partner would be proportionately responsible for covering the difference. If the home needed repairs, each of the partners would be responsible, again in proportion to the original investment that each made and the corresponding percentage of the profits to which each was entitled.

Note that in a joint venture the partner's commitment doesn't end with the original investment. Debts and unforeseen expenses are an ongoing liability for which the partners are responsible.

That concept of responsibility is the key in differentiating between joint ventures and limited partnerships, in which the investor's liability is limited to the amount originally put forth.

Limited partnerships take one of two forms, either private or public. Private partnerships have no more than thirty-five partners. A greater number means that the partnership automatically is public. Investors in private partnerships usually have the right to vote on major decisions faced by the partnership. In a real estate private partnership, for example, the limited partners would be able to decide whether to acquire a certain building, whether or not to refinance it, and when to sell it. Investors in public partnerships haven't even that privilege, because of the logistical problems involved in polling the opinions of a large group of people.

In either case, the daily decisions and responsibilities rest with a *general partner* who is, in effect, the manager of the partnership. He or she is paid either by a management fee commission at the beginning of the deal, or, much preferably, by a smaller fee and a percentage of any profits when the partnership ends. (Common sense tells you that the latter method, sometimes known as "sweat equity," provides much more incentive for the general partner to work for a maximum profit.)

You might wonder why an investor would want to give up the right to participate in the management of the partnership. The answer is that many investors don't want the responsibility of running the project, that they lack the knowledge that property management requires. There is almost no demand on the time on a limited partner, since someone else is being paid to run the project and make the decisions.

More important, limited partners probably will never be called to pump in more money to keep the project alive. The goals and the principles are clearly stated beforehand. The limited partner knows what the partnership will have to work with, how much is to be spent, and (at least generally) where the money is to go. In buying into a limited partnership, an investor gives up most of his or her rights to govern the partnership in return for a specific percentage of any possible profits and the knowledge that the project will be conducted according to the manner specified in the prospectus.

For its own purposes, the Internal Revenue Service defines limited partnerships as distinct from corporations. (The tax structures are different for each.) According to the IRS, a corporation is characterized by:

—Continuity of life. Corporations are designed to exist indefinitely, while limited partnerships are drawn up with a specific limit on their existence.

—Centralization of authority, meaning that a few people are responsible for the vital decisions of the project. This is true of corporations, which usually have boards of directors and management staffs, and it is usually the case with partnerships as well, in which a few general partners are entrusted with running the project.

—Limited liability. Again, this applies to both corporations and limited partnerships. Stockholders' liability is limited to the value of the shares they own in a corporation, while limited partners are obligated only to the extent of the money they already have paid into the partnership.

—Free transfer of interest. This is a characteristic of corporations whose shares are traded on the open market and can be bought and sold easily. Partnerships, however, restrict the partners' rights to sell their interest in the project. Most of the partnerships in which I have taken a role, as either a limited or a general partner, permit transfer of ownership only through inheritance or divorce.

According to the IRS, any group business venture satisfying at least three of those requirements is classified as a corporation. You'll note that limited partnerships can be expected to meet only two of the criteria. For that reason, in order to retain the tax benefits of being able to pass operating losses straight through to the individual partners, limited partnerships are structured strictly to observe the limited period of life and the nontransferability of interest.

Limited partnerships have been proposed in probably every field of business endeavor, partly for business reasons and party for tax benefits. The IRS allows these special benefits in order to stimulate business and involve a greater number of investors in the business community. Real estate is a popular area for partnerships. The production of coal and the exploration and development of oil and gas are others.

Oil and gas partnerships are among the longer-lived of those available. (The longest partnership term in which I've been personally involved was for forty years and was a real estate renovation; many partnerships are given fairly long lives to allow the general partner flexibility, so it's common for a partnership to end before the term expires. The shortest I know of is a gem-buying partnership structured to last just one year.) Oil and gas projects are of three types: exploratory, developmental, and a combination of both.

Exploratory partnerships are extremely risky. If the partnership company should find what it is seeking, then the returns will be quick and probably generous. But there is a good chance that no worthwhile discoveries will be made, in which case the partners sustain a major loss. Because of the risky aspects of this kind of venture, IRS rules permit a first-year write-off of as much as 90 percent of the investment, depending on how many commissions have been paid.

Developmental partnerships are formed to produce oil and gas from fields that already have been discovered and judged worthwhile. The risk to the investors is far less than with exploratory partnerships, but the tax advantages are minimal and so are the possibilities of a huge profit. Several developmental partnerships show a return of 12 to 15 percent within the first fifteen months of their existence. Cash flow is usually quite regular, with quarterly payoffs.

I favor the combination partnership, which has elements of both exploratory and developmental work. I try to steer my clients toward projects that are weighted toward the developmental side, 60-40 or 70-30. This still leaves the opportunity for big profits from an unexpected strike by exploratory crews, while the developmental work ensures a steady income to keep the enterprise healthy. These combination programs also offer a write-off of approximately 80 percent of the investment the first year, so that an investment of $5,000 would allow a $4,000 write-off as partnership losses on the next return.

I've found that such projects are reliable about reporting their progress to investors. The quarterly disbursal of funds tends to be dependable, since the general partners establish a reserve of funds for unproductive and unprofitable periods. Once they begin the payment of quarterly profits, they don't like to stop.

These partnerships end when the oil and gas is gone. In real estate, the end comes with the selling of the properties that the partnership originally was formed to develop. (Real estate partnerships ought to be structured so as to forbid the general partners from selling one of the original buildings and using the money to buy another later during the life of the partnership.) Private real estate partnerships are formed to develop a single property; public real estate partnerships usually include several properties in their portfolios. As each individual property is sold, the proceeds should be distributed at that time to the partners.

Agriculture has been an increasingly popular field for partnerships—fruit and nut trees, pistachios, vineyards. There is considerable risk attached to many of these projects, since much depends on climatic variables.

Movies and records used to be very popular objects for partnerships since they offered tax write-offs several times the size of the original investment. But the Tax Law of 1976, which specified that an investor can write off no more than the amount for which he or she is actually at risk, ended such abuses, and rightfully so, for many projects were created purposely to fail. Tax write-offs, not profits, were the aim of many of these enterprises.

As a result of the reform, movies and records are not as popular as they used to be for partnerships. They still retain a glamorous appeal, however. As a result, investors are sometimes less particular about these partnerships than they would be with more mundane products. For example, I discovered that one of my clients had "lent" $20,000 to a movie production. He knew little about the production, had no idea what the risks might be or what percentage of the profits he might expect to receive. In fact, he was so blinded by the aura of the movie business that he knew almost nothing about the investment he had just made.

On his behalf, I attended an investors' meeting held by the production company. Of the approximately twenty-five investors there, only two—including me—asked any questions pertinent to the financial particulars of this deal. For the others, this expensive proximity to the movie business apparently was sufficient. My client lost every penny of his money.

To prevent such abuses, the Securities Exchange Commission has set up stringent disclosure rules for all public partnerships. (Private partnerships aren't bound by the same rules, but you ought to expect the same standards of a private partnership that the SEC sets for public ones. Regulation of private partnerships tends to be after the fact, when someone complains about improper practices. Investors in private partnerships have some degree of assurance if a general partner is required to obtain a state permit for the line of business in which he or she is engaged. This ensures a certain amount of scrutiny, but no guarantees.)

The result of the SEC regulations can be seen in the complicated subscription form and voluminous prospectus that every public partnership now issues. These are drawn up by skilled legal and accounting experts who specialize in helping partnerships meet the requirements of full disclosure regulations.

The size of the documents may be a bit frightening; don't be intimidated. Much of the information is included simply to satisfy legal requirements for the formal protection of investors. For example, the prospectus for every partnership that I have helped to form contains a standard clause to the effect that while the partnership is structured to take advantage of existing tax laws, those laws could change and the investors could lose their tax benefits. That seems obvious to most of the people who read the prospectus, for tax laws change frequently. But full disclosure requires that facts be brought out anyway, no matter how obvious they may seem.

The paragraphs that follow, then, are both an explanation of some of the more important portions of the prospectus and a discussion of what you should expect to find there. They are the standards that you should apply when judging the partnership.

Every partnership ought to specify the names of the general partners, their previous experience, and the record of any partnerships in which they have previously been involved.

This is crucial for a number of reasons. You need to know, first of all, that the people involved are professional, capable people who know the fine points of the type of investment they are planning. You need to be confident, for example, that you are getting accurate and timely tax information for your own returns and that the project is structured to satisfy the requirements of a limited partnership. A faulty return submitted by the partnership can mean an audit of the returns of all the limited partners and can seriously jeopardize some of the tax benefits they have claimed.

It is also important that the general partners establish themselves as reputable business people who are forming this partnership for the profits that may accrue, not simply to take an immediate slice out of the money raised from investors. There is a great deal of money being made in partnerships today, and any profitable activity is bound to attract its share of hustlers and con artists. Consider that general partners and selling agents often take a cut of 20 percent or more from the sum originally raised from the sale of limited partnership units. In a million-dollar partnership— not so rare these days—that percentage amounts to $200,000, which is plenty of encouragement for a hustler.

To protect yourself from a swindle in a real estate partnership, personally inspect the property that the group plans to buy. In the renovation projects involving private partnerships in which I am the general partner, limited partners are encouraged to see the property as it appears when we buy it, at its worst. Then we update the project periodically with photographs to show the partners what progress is being made with their money. Finally, when the renovation is complete, we host a wine-and-cheese party on the premises of the remodeled building before the tenants move in.

In addition, the books and records of the partnership should be available for the partners' inspection during normal business hours, at a specific place. It might be useful to know which banks the partnership uses for its accounts.

I mentioned that the accounting ought to be done by experts familiar with partnerships. This is crucial, since an average of one of every four partnership returns is audited by the IRS. In addition, the general partner ought to be able to provide you with a reasonably accurate outline of the tax benefits you can expect within the last quarter of every year. This is helpful in tax planning. You should be notified if the benefits appear to be out of line with what was anticipated, because in that case you may want to make some adjustments in other areas to compensate for the difference.

The IRS requires only that partnerships file a K-1 return by April 15. A K-1 form is the partnership's return that is filed on behalf of the partnership in April, similar to an individual 1040A form. In reality, those forms ought to come to you earlier than that, so that you may have a chance to complete your personal return. If the K-1 forms are late, the IRS will grant a sixty-day extension for your personal return, if you file a form asking for it.

Besides the identities of the general partners and important staff members and a listing of their qualifications and track records, the prospectus also must state the existence of any litigation, pending or resolved, that might affect the performance of the partnership. It ought to mention any fact that might be detrimental to the successful outcome of the partnership and any risk factors that can be foreseen. If the partnership will be dealing with a specific broker or sales agency, that fact should be mentioned, along with the size of the commission to be paid.

Because a private partnership deals with a single project, its prospectus should include a detailed expenditure sheet showing exactly how much money is to be taken in and exactly how it is to be spent. In a private real estate partnership, for example, the prospectus (sometimes called an "offering memorandum") should describe in detail what percentage of the money is to be spent on different aspects of construction and renovation, and when.

Public partnerships cannot be so detailed, because they almost always involve several projects, the nature of which may not be known at the time of the offering. Instead, the money will be broken down into just a few general items. But the prospectus should tell how the general partners are to be compensated, as well as how much money is to be raised and how many partnership units are to be sold. This guarantees a specific maximum number of partners and it ensures that each partnership unit will receive a specific percentage of the eventual profits. For instance, partnerships needing $1,000,000 for a project might sell 100 units at $10,000 apiece. A limited partner owning one partnership unit would be guaranteed one one-hundredth, or 1 percent, of all the profits turned back to the limited partners.

Partnerships will require a minimum net worth, or a minimum earnings capability—or both—of any potential investor. This is to prevent unsophisticated and unqualified investors from getting into something they don't understand or can't really afford. This isn't snobbery; the fact is that there is an element of risk in every partnership project. Investors who can absorb a loss are less likely to be hurt than those who have lost money they desperately needed.

For the same reason, investors are required to sign a statement on the partnership subscription form certifying that they have read the prospectus and understand it, that they are aware of the risks involved, and that they can afford to take the risk. Another clause in the subscription agreement urges the would-be buyer to seek professional counseling before deciding to invest in the project.

You can save yourself a good deal of wading through the legal tangle of the prospectus by skipping straight to the portion that outlines the objectives and principles of the partnership. Unless you agree with the guidelines stated there, you need not take the trouble to read any more.

A real estate partnership prospectus might state that the only objective is to buy townhouses in certain affluent areas, paying 40 percent down. If that rather conservative objective doesn't appeal to you, you can eliminate that particular deal.

In addition to the statement about the amount of money to be raised, the prospectus may also specify a minimum figure, a so-called "effective amount," with which the partnership can be started. An oil and gas partnership may try to raise $10,000,000. But the prospectus may state an effective amount of $8,000,000. The additional $2,000,000 is helpful, but not necessary, in achieving the goals of the partnership.

You might be interested in the way two actual partnerships in real estate were formed, how they were structured, and the results they achieved.

The first example is a renovation project involving a three-story, 3,600-square foot building, vintage 1876. Though the building had been badly neglected, it still retained much of its original charm. The objective was to renovate the building totally and reconstruct it so that it would be suitable for leasing as professional offices. The partners hoped to make a profit from the rental revenues, from tax benefits, from refinancing, and from the eventual sale of the property with its greatly increased value.

The purchase price of the property was $117,000. The partners were able to assume a $46,000 mortgage and got a second mortgage of $51,000 to cover the rest of the price.

The general partners raised $170,000 (from 17 units of $10,000 each), with the investors to receive 70 percent of the profits. The $170,000 covered $110,000 for the renovation costs, debt service on the two mortgages, legal and accounting fees, taxes, and cash reserves of about $27,000.

There was no income during the first year of the partnership. Because of this, and because of the expense of renovation, plus the Investment Tax Credit that the IRS allows for buildings over twenty years old, the tax benefits yielded about a 30 percent write-off that year for the investors, or around $3,000 for each $10,000 investment.

Leases for the second year, after the renovation was finished, brought 95 cents per square foot per month, or $3,420 a month, $41,040 per year. This gave the partnership a basis for approaching banks at the end of the second year for refinancing, since the rental income had been more than sufficient to carry the $117,000 original mortgage debt. The advantage to refinancing can be multiple—it increases tax deductions due to increased mortgage payments and allows for money or equity that is considered "dead" to be withdrawn for other purposes, possibly additional investments, without declaring any taxable gains. The bank that eventually was chosen for refinancing appraised the property and approved a $200,000 refinance loan. (The partners had turned down an offer of $225,000 for the property during renovation.) Again, the lease revenues were enough to cover the cost of that mortgage payment. The original $46,000 mortgage and the newer $51,000 second mortgage both were paid off, leaving $103,000 in funds.

Commonly in limited partnerships, the limited partners receive 99 percent of proceeds until their original investment has been returned. The practice held true in this instance, so the general partners received just $1,030 of the original proceeds, while the remaining 99 percent, or $101,970, was divided among the limited partners.

Meanwhile, cash flow had begun from the lease. Maintenance was minimal because of the new plumbing and electrical systems that had been installed. The general partners charged a 5 percent management fee of $2,052 per year. Legal and accounting costs were another $2,500 per year. About $30,000 per year was available for debt service, but lease rates increased 8 percent at the beginning of the second year of leasing and were increased again another 7 percent at the beginning of the third year of leasing, when the building was put on the market. So the rental income the second year of leasing was increased to $44,323. Income for the third year of leasing was projected at $47,425. This gave the limited partners a positive cash flow (rare in partnerships); with refinancing, by the end of the second year, the limited partners had regained 89 percent of their original investment. (This is counting the $3,000 tax break they received from write-offs the first year.) The remaining 11 percent was made up by excess cash flow from the rental revenues.

The building was put up for sale during the second year of

occupancy, the third year of the project's existence (counting a year during which the building was vacant and renovation took place). Rental rates were increased the additional 7 percent to project higher income and make the property more attractive; the building was sold for $450,000. Of this amount, $199,000 went to pay off the refinancing loan and $11,250 satisfied the prepayment penalty. Another 4 percent, or $18,000 was paid out as a commission to the real estate broker. This left $221,750 in profits, of which 70 percent, or $155,225, was returned to the limited partners. This represented a 91.3 percent return after the original money had been repaid, so each $10,000 investment showed a $9,130 profit. This was taxed as long-term capital gains, so the maximum tax that each partner would have paid was $2,556 on a $10,000 investment.

The second example, involving the purchase and resale of an apartment house, is even more spectacularly successful.

Bought in February 1979 and sold fourteen months later in April 1980, the building consisted of ninety-six units, sixty-three of which were two-bedroom, two-bath apartments that rented for $230 a month at the time of purchase. The remaining thirty-three units were one-bedroom, one-bath, and rented for $180 per month at the time of purchase. There was a 10 percent vacancy rate. With those figures alone, the general partner projected $220,644 in rental income for a year. (See illustration, page 162.)

The building sold for $1,500,000, or about 6.8 times gross earnings. This was in an area where the gross multiplier for other apartments ranged up to 8.5 times annual gross rents. The general partner decided that the gross multiplier could be increased at the time of resale and that rents could be raised significantly if the building were upgraded with landscaping, painting, and recarpeting. This did, in fact, take place after the building was purchased.

The $1,500,000 purchase price, which included closing costs, was raised by a $1,000,000 first mortgage, a $250,000 second trust deed from the seller (for five years, interest only at 10 percent), and $350,000 raised from limited partners in $10,000 units. This totaled $1,600,000. The excess $100,000

Apartment House—Limited Partnership

Purchased in February 1979
Sold in April 1980

Original cost	$1,500,000 net (including clos- ing costs)
First mortgage	$1,000,000 @ 9¾%
Second to fifth year mortgage from owner	$ 250,000 @ 10%—interest only
Investment from limited partners	$ 350,000
	$1,600,000

($100,000 will be used for upgrading units and reserves.)
Ten-year-old building, consisting of ninety-six units, sixty-three, 2-bedroom, 2-bath and thirty-three one bedroom, 1 bath. Original rents:

2-bedroom @ $230 per month
1-bedroom @ $180 per month

There is a 10 per cent vacancy factor, Complex was bought at just under 7 times gross income.

$230 × 63 units = $14,490 per month × 12 = $173,880
$180 × 33 units = $5940 per month × 12 = $71,280

$173,880
+ 71,280
$245,160 gross rent
− 24,516 10 percent vacancy factor
$220,644 adjusted gross income

Dividing the sales price by net income yields:

$$\frac{1,500,000}{220,644} = 6.8$$

was set aside for the upgrading expenses and a small cash reserve.

The upgrading was done during the fourteen months that the partnership owned the building. During this period rents gradually were raised to $250 and $310, respectively, for the one-bedroom and two-bedroom units. This brought about a change in the tenant profile, resulting in a vacancy rate of just 4 percent. The cash flow during the fourteen months went to debt service and maintenance. (The remainder was passed back to the limited partners.)

The increased rents, a decreased vacancy rate, and a larger gross multiplier of 8 allowed the general partner to get a price of $2,600,000 in April 1980, as the following figures indicate:

$$2\text{-bedroom @ } \$310 \text{ per month}$$
$$1\text{-bedroom @ } \$250 \text{ per month}$$

$310 × 63 units = $19,530 × 12 = $234,360
$250 × 33 units = $ 8,250 × 12 = $ 99,000

$234,360
+ 99,000
—————
$333,360 gross income
−   .04   vacancy rate $333,360
—————   − 13,334
$ 13,334.40   —————
                                $320,026 NET

$320,026
×   8 gross multiplier
—————
$2,560,208

The proceeds of the sale went to pay off the two loan balances, a prepayment penalty for the first mortgage, and a real estate commission, with proceeds of $1,199,000. (See chart.) The original $350,000 was returned to the limited partners, leaving a cash distribution available of $849,000. The original partnership agreement stated that after the limited partners received their original equity back in cash (this does not take into account any tax benefits), the limited partners would receive 70 percent of remaining profits, the general partners 30 percent. The limited partners received a total of $594,300, which, divided by the thirty-five investment units, yielded a cash return of $16,980 per unit, or nearly 170 percent profit. The general partners received 30 percent of that, or $254,700. At current rates, maximum tax on this long-term gain was 28 percent, giving each investor an after-tax profit of $12,226, or 122 percent, on each original $10,000 investment after just fourteen months. (An investor would have to be in the 70 percent tax bracket to pay the 28 percent tax.)

Selling price was $2,600,000:

$2,600,000	
⟨ 999,000 ⟩	Loan balance first mortgage
⟨ $ 48,000 ⟩	Penalty on prepayment of loan (approximately six months' interest)
⟨ $ 250,000 ⟩	Second mortgage to previous owner
⟨ $ 104,000 ⟩	Real Estate commission, 4 percent (large commission should be negotiated)
$1,199,000	cash proceeds
	$1,199,000 net proceeds
	⟨ $ 350,000 ⟩ original limited partners' capital
$ 849,000	

$254,700 General Partners = 30%
$ 594,300 = Limited partners' share of profits
−350,000 = Limited partners' original equity
$ 944,300 = Total cash return to limited partners

Investors received original money plus 170 percent cash return in a little over one year. Maximum tax will be 28 percent ($594,300 × .28) or $166,404 for the entire partnership. This of course will vary per individual according to her tax bracket when she declares the gain for the respective tax year.

Limited partners should always get their original capital back first, before the general partners takes their percentage split, which is determined before the project is started.

To calculate what a $10,000 investment will make:
$10,000 Original investment
$16,980 170 percent profit
$ 4,754 Maximum tax @ 70 percent tax bracket
($16,980 × .28)
$16,980
$ 4,754
$12,226 = Minimum return after taxes, 122 percent profit

If the investor had been single and had had a taxable income of $23,500 (which would put her in a 39 percent tax bracket), her tax obligation on the long-term gain of $16,980 would be calculated as follows:
$16,980
× .40
$ 6,792 (Portion to be taxed at taxpayer's personal bracket)
$ 6,792
× .39 (Taxpayer's bracket)
$ 2,649 Tax due

In long-term capital gains (over one-year holding period), the IRS currently excludes 60 percent of the profit, thus taxing 40 percent of the gain at the taxpayer's tax bracket, with a maximum tax paid of 28 percent. When a taxpayer is obligated to pay this maximum tax of 28 percent, that means she is in the 70 percent bracket.

Don't be intimidated by the 28 percent maximum tax and

the 70 percent bracket that I keep mentioning. To be in this position, you would need the following taxable income:

Single	$103,300
Married	$215,400
Head of household	$161,300

To determine the overall taxable gain, a portion of the depreciation (that which was in excess of straight-line depreciation) will be recaptured and declared. In addition, improvements that were capitalized and not expensed (capitalized in this instance means that the overall improvement may be spread out over three to five years—e.g., $10,000 in carpet divided by 5, which equals $2,000 per year) will be declared in full. Quite often in the selling of a project within a short period of time—approximately two years—recaptured expenses may offset excess depreciation, as it did in the above illustration.

Despite high personal tax brackets, many of the original investors did not feel the full effects of the 28 percent tax. Even though the property was sold and not exchanged, as is commonly done to defer the gains tax, the sale occurred early enough in the year that most investors were able to reinvest their profits into other enterprises offering write-offs that helped to diminish their tax liability.

Limited partnerships can come in all sizes and shapes. As you begin to make investments you will find that potential investments surround you. Stock brokerage firms across the country offer public limited partnerships to their clients, and they may even sponsor a seminar for a specific partnership they are promoting. This may give you an opportunity to find out what the product is, what kind of track record the general partners have, what the minimum dollar participation is, and how many years your dollars are likely to be tied up, along with the answers to any other questions that may occur to you. Brokerage firms offer a variety of products that may include real estate, oil and gas, leasing, cattle, agriculture, flowers, research and development, and many others.

My company has sponsored programs that involved gems, antiques, art, oil and gas, business opportunities, real estate (both developmental and commercial), historical renovations, and even a pub.

A prospectus for a public offering (definitely more than thirty-five investors) can be obtained on request from any brokerage firm that is participating in the offering. You can also request the prospectus directly from the general partners, if they are known to you.

If you do request a prospectus, be aware that a salesperson will call you, possibly numerous times, to encourage you to purchase a unit. If you go directly to the general partners, they will give your name to a salesperson who is participating in the program. Remember, their goal is to sell the product, the sooner the better.

In a private offering (from one to thirty-five investors) prospectuses will not be mailed out to everyone who requests one.

Companies that offer or sponsor private offerings must keep close supervision on who the potential investors are that have requested prospectuses, who has returned them, and who has invested. If they didn't keep such close tabs and mailed a prospectus to just anyone who asked for one, the offering would no longer be private.

The policy of my company is that no one can receive a prospectus of a private offering without having a consultation with one of our planners. By doing this, we are able to determine whether a client is suitable for a particular investment as well as what his or her objectives and goals are and whether they are realistic.

Often we have seen a group of acquaintances pool their dollars and begin investing together, the final objective being to sell at a higher price than was originally paid.

During the gasoline price increases in late 1979 and early

1980, a friend of mine was astute enough to order several Honda cars. In California, those cars sold for more than the suggested retail price. My friend resold them by putting an ad in the local papers and made almost $1,000 per car. Her original deposit when ordering them had been $500 each. Can you imagine what she might have done if she had pooled her resources with several other investors and bought many more cars to resell?

Investments, whether undertaken on your own or as a member of a limited partnership, can be imaginative, innovative, and profitable.

10

PLANNING A FINANCIAL STRATEGY

An old saying has it that there are only two things in life that are guaranteed: death and taxes. In putting together your financial plan, you must take those two elements into account, along with your marital status, personal objectives, willingness to take risks, financial resources, and income needs—and, of course, the state of the economy.

Your plan will vary according to your marital status. Today's woman has a choice of marrying, living with a partner while remaining unmarried, or living single and alone. She may experience all three in a few years. Each change in status will influence her financial decisions.

From a purely legal and financial standpoint, the simplest of the three options is to remain single and unattached. Moreover, the single woman and the divorced woman without children often seem to be freer and more aggressive in making investments. In a thesis that I completed in the spring of 1980 for my MBA degree, I studied a large group of women—married, single, and divorced—to explore women's investment problems. One of my findings was that single and divorced women tended to be much more risk-oriented and more likely to use financial advisers than their married counterparts. This supports the commonly held theory that married women tend to abdicate much of their share of important decision making to their husbands.

At the same time, single women are sometimes freer to make important decisions that affect their lifestyles. You may recall my example in Chapters 2 and 3 of a young woman who moved closer to her job, began spending evenings at home, and embarked on a crash program to save money and qualify to take out a loan for investments. Such radical changes are more difficult if two or more people are involved, especially if one of the parties is not as committed to the new way of doing things.

Employed young women who are making just a moderate amount of money are often very independent, responsible, and aware of investment possibilities. Yet they frequently lack specific knowledge and expertise, as was shown in my study: While 90 percent of the women I interviewed had at least some college education, only 5 percent had any background in finance or economics.

I feel that one of the most important priorities for women, whether they are single women who have sole responsibility for decision making or married women who want to begin playing a larger role, is to acquire the tools and education necessary to explore investments and financial opportunities. This can pay off in innumerable ways; it can even help you to save money on commissions and advisory fees.

If you are a single woman, your strategy should include putting money aside for savings, some of which will eventually become capital for investments. Probably there will be considerable room to cut down on entertainment and incidentals. Decide what is more important—having a good time, or increasing your net worth. It's very possible that you can have room for both. Restrict yourself, but not in a straitjacket. I repeat what I have emphasized before: Know your goals, and know what you have to do to achieve them. Plan ahead. In some cases, you may have to extend the time limit you've originally given yourself; for example, it may take you more than a year of planning and budgeting to buy into a condominium, to purchase a new car, or to procure a painting.

The most important advice I have for the single, career-oriented woman is to be constantly aware of taxes and what they are doing to your investment power.

The woman in a living-together arrangement may be in a sort of limbo, sharing the freedoms and responsibilities of both single and married women. Much depends on the specifics of the relationship, on the way the couple has defined it. Some arrangements are virtual marriages without the wedding ceremony. Others are far less formal, with fewer demands and expectations.

The woman in such a relationship will probably be working, with a career. It is not likely that she will have children during the term of the arrangement, though this is becoming more common. And she may have children from an earlier marriage or relationship. Since she will not file a joint tax return, she needs to evaluate her itemized deductions closely, recognizing she won't be getting any tax benefits from anyone but herself.

On the other hand, she won't be getting any tax liabilities from anyone else, either. Some couples in this situation are planning marriage. They ought to look at their combined incomes and the tax consequences if they marry near the end of the year. An individual's filing status for *an entire year* is determined by his or her marital status on December 31 of that year. Very often marriage brings a tax penalty that can be avoided for a year by postponing marriage until early the following year. One of my clients saved $4,000 in taxes on a combined income of $70,000 by postponing the wedding from the last week in December to the first week in January.

A couple that remains in a living-together arrangement without marriage may have the united purpose and goals of a married couple, planning together and not as individuals. Whether or not this is the way your arrangement works, you may want to have a legal document drawn up that clearly defines who owns which property in case the relationship is dissolved. Such a document is similar to a prenuptial agreement that restricts the amount of property or alimony a partner can get in the event of divorce. Recent court decisions have clearly established that unmarried live-in partners have property rights, especially in longer relationships, so such an advance agreement has become more and more important.

Insurance needs of single women and those who are living with men are usually minimal unless they have children or other dependents who need their continued financial support. Except in those instances, the group insurance that their employers may carry is likely to be sufficient. Later in the chapter I'll discuss the value of insurance for married couples, especially as a means of estate planning.

As common as divorce has become, coping with it is never easy. For many women the difficulties of regrouping emotionally are compounded by the need to initiate and carry through a financial plan for the first time in their lives.

No woman ought to find herself in quite this devastating a position. As I discussed in the first chapter, the great majority of women will be solely responsible for their financial well-being at some stage in their lives, so I cannot urge too strongly that all women, married and single, prepare themselves now to handle their money intelligently.

In mapping out a financial strategy after a divorce, a woman should look at several factors. First, she should decide how long it will take her to begin making a salary on which she can support herself, care for her dependents if any, maintain her lifestyle, and begin long-range financial planning. She may have been out of the work force for a long time, so she may be far away from achieving the salary she needs. In that case she may want to take some of the proceeds from the divorce settlement and invest them to produce income.

She may have received a lump sum of cash as part of the settlement. If so, she should remember the effects of inflation on money that lies unused. She may have received a house as part of the settlement, perhaps with the stipulation that it must be sold when the youngest child reaches age eighteen. If this is the case she may not wind up netting all the money that she anticipates, for capital taxes will eat into the profits unless she buys a house with a higher price, which a woman often can't afford because she doesn't make enough income to qualify for a loan that large.

Remember that deaths and divorces are often publicized, especially where large sums of money are involved. A woman recently widowed or divorced should be careful not to become prey to unscrupulous counselors who specialize in pursuing the business of recently widowed and divorced women. Always check out the people with whom you're dealing, and don't be swayed by persistence (especially at a time when you may be especially vulnerable). Demand references and then verify them. Ask friends who have been in similar circumstances for referrals, including the names of professionals whom your friends have been unhappy with and why.

As always, when you plan investments, you should be aware of exactly what is producing the best results (in terms of current income and growth) and what the effects of inflation will be. The goals should be a sustained income that will supply annual revenue, while the capital maintains its value against the slumping value of the dollar.

If money is tied up in high-yield stocks with dividends (which usually have minimal growth), interest-paying bonds, or certificates of deposit (which do provide income), inflation may erode the value of the principal. Use the guidelines I've mentioned earlier for choosing and evaluating stocks. Since predictable income is the goal, you'll probably want to eliminate any stock that has had rough periods during which dividends were reduced or suspended.

The necessity of having a solid plan is all the more important given the recent trend in divorce settlements, which have dramatically pared down the amount of support that former husbands must pay and the length of time they must pay it. It is far less frequent now than it used to be for a wife to be granted large spousal support payments for an indefinite period. It is now quite common for women who are divorced after as long as twenty years of marriage to be granted only five years of alimony, and for any money that they make during that period to be used to offset part of the husband's monthly obligation.

My experience of widows is that they usually face either a feast or a famine. If there has been proper planning, they have time to retrain themselves as wage earners, to evaluate their financial situation properly, and to make sober investments. The alternative is panic and distress, which can occur even in families with a high net worth. One widow whom I advised was left assets in commercial real estate totaling more than $1,000,000. But her husband had not planned to leave a reserve of liquid assets and had failed to understand that there could be a substantial tax liability. The widow had to sell her properties at distressed value, with the result that her husband's actual legacy was much smaller than he'd ever anticipated. Since few widows will ever have such assets, proper planning is even more critical.

Husband and wife should do this planning together. The way to begin is to find out about the property laws regarding married couples in the state in which you live. If you now live—or during the course of your marriage have lived for any significant length of time—in one of the eight community-property states (California, Nevada, Idaho, Washington, Texas, Louisiana, New Mexico, and Arizona), you should know that property acquired by the partners during the marriage is likely to be regarded as community property unless it is specifically recorded as being otherwise. If your spouse should die, items that are solely your own may become subject to probate. (Probate is the court-officiated settlement of the deceased's will.)

How do you distinguish?

Anything owned by you before marriage is your separate property. Anything acquired by gift to you during marriage is your separate property. Property that was acquired in a state that did not have community property is judged according to the laws of that state.

Some states stipulate that income acquired by the wife is separate property. In addition, income derived from separate property—like rental income, for example, from a home that you inherited from one of your relatives—is separate property.

This could cause problems because money from separate property that is spent as community money could be considered a gift from one spouse to another, and federal law provides for a gift tax on any sum over $3,000 per person per year.

Property acquired as a result of the sale of separate property is also separate property. Let's say that as a child you were given a painting for your birthday. The painter becomes famous, the painting becomes valuable, and you marry. The painting is separate property. If you should sell the painting and buy 100 shares of IBM, that stock is also separate property, and so is the dividend income. And if you sell the IBM stock, whatever you buy with the proceeds is still separate property.

If that sounds complicated, it sometimes is. The laws vary from state to state, and the character of each piece of property is determined by when and how it was acquired, and in which state you were a resident when that occurred.

The only way to deal coherently with the subject is to keep a list of all important assets, with notations about the date and method of acquisition and sale. In addition, note what was done with the proceeds. In case of death or divorce, it may become necessary to trace the ownership of each piece of property belonging to you and your spouse.

In addition, there are inheritance taxes to concern you. In recent years, federal law has raised the amount of property that can be passed on without tax to approximately $175,000 in 1981. Some states, unfortunately, have not followed the example, while other states have minimal or zero estate taxes. If your spouse dies, you don't want to be paying taxes on something that actually is your property, but the co-mingling of assets that inevitably occurs in marriage sometimes makes it inevitable.

One solution may be life insurance, especially when you

have assets that are nonliquid. You may have gathered from earlier chapters that I'm not impressed with the value of life insurance as an investment. But it can be one way to deal with estate problems, and it may be your only way of providing for those who depend upon your income for their financial well-being.

My advice is for husband and wife to own life insurance policies on one another, each paying for the policies with funds that are clearly separate property. The policies themselves (proceeds of separate property) are likewise separate property and can only be taxed in the owner's estate, not the insured's. That means that the surviving spouse owns the policy outright. It is not subject to probate, and the money paid under the policy can be used to help pay inheritance taxes without forcing a distressed sale of other properties or valuables.

The amount of insurance you need should be based on the property that may be taxable in case of death and on how many people depend upon you and the income you generate. If you don't have dependents, there's a high probability that you don't need insurance at all. If you are receiving alimony or child support payments, you might consider taking out a policy on the life of the individual responsible for those payments. If he should die the payments would stop, but the insurance policy would provide the money that can be so essential, especially for the costs of bringing up a child.

There are basically two types of kinds of insurance, *term* and *whole life*. When you are talking with an insurance agent, he or she may offer you what seems to be a vast array of types of insurance. There are lots of fancy names with different types of window dressing, but they are still term and whole-life insurance.

Term insurance is pure insurance. It offers a set amount of money to the beneficiary of the policy if the insured dies. You pay for one year's insurance at a time. In annual renewal term, the cost increases each year because you are one year closer to dying according to the mortality tables. It's very similar to car and home insurance. If something catastrophic happens, you know that coverage is there. Few of us really feel that we can do without basic insurance on our homes, cars, etc., although we may complain about costs increasing. Term life insurance works in pretty much the same way. The older you get, the more the cost increases. It is substantially lower in premium cost than whole life because there is no savings account tied into it.

Whole-life insurance is a combination of protection plus a savings program. The policy may be for a total amount of, for example, $50,000. Each year the owner of the policy pays her premium. As each year goes by, she begins to accrue a savings account. The life insurance company that the policy is held with has agreed to pay the beneficiary the amount of $50,000 if the insured dies, and no more than that amount. If savings amount to $2,000, that means that the insurance company returns the $2,000 plus $48,000 from them, totaling $50,000. You do not get the face amount of the policy ($50,000) plus the savings. Some women feel that this is a good way to build a savings account.

I fully disagree. Term insurance will be far less expensive for a woman under the age of forty-five than whole-life insurance. If you have children, I would advise you to purchase the amount of insurance that is necessary to provide an income that will take care of your dependents until they reach maturity or until your spouse or selected guardian can support them as you feel is appropriate. In addition, when your attorney is reviewing your will and/or you have an update interview with your accountant or financial planner, you should estimate the taxes on your estate. If you or your estate will not have the cash to pay the estate taxes, term insurance should be considered.

Costs will vary substantially from company to company. Make sure that you get at least three quotes. A guideline you might use is that for a woman who is thirty, a $100,000 annual renewable policy (means renewed each year without new physical) should be approximately $205.

⟨$100,000 ANNUAL RENEWABLE TERM
POLICY⟩

Age	
25	$195
30	205
35	215
40	250
45	350
50	530
55	825
60	1275

You can see in the above that costs increase substantially as you get older, which makes sense according to actuarial tables. Over the age of sixty, increases in premiums are substantial, but I am assuming that you won't have any dependents who are minors at that time of your life.

Whole-life rates will vary even more than term rates in initial premiums. Once a standard whole-life policy is in force, the annual premium remains constant. Do remember that there is a savings account tacked on, but at a 5 to 6 percent interest rate for policies dated after 1978 and 2½ to 3 percent for policies dated before 1978.

As I mentioned earlier, the premiums for term insurance increase as you grow older, while premiums for whole-life insurance do not. The reason that the cost of a whole-life policy remains constant is that, as the cash value increases each year, the insurance side actually decreases. For example, in the accompanying chart, a thirty-year-old woman can purchase $100,000 of whole-life insurance for $968 a year. In twenty years (when she is fifty years old), the policy will have accrued a minimum cash value of $22,300. She originally contracted for $100,000 in coverage. If you deduct the cash value of $22,300 from $100,000, the difference is $77,700. Thus, the insurance company needs to cover the insured with only $77,700, not the full $100,000. Because of the reduced

Sample Whole-Life Policy

($100,000 coverage)

Minimum Cash Value

Begin-ning Age	Premium Amount	After 5 Years	After 10 Years	After 15 Years	After 20 Years
25	$ 795/yr.	$1100	$ 7300	$12,500	$18,500
30	968/yr.	1880	9100	15,300	22,300
35	1195/yr.	2990	11,150	18,500	26,500
40	1495/yr.	3980	13,400	22,000	31,000
45	1885/yr.	5170	15,950	25,700	35,700
50	2380/yr.	6175	18,700	29,700	40,500
55	3010/yr.	7875	21,700	33,800	45,050
60	3875/yr.	9500	24,800	37,550	49,300

actual coverage, the premium does not increase even though the insured has increased in age.

Probate is almost always difficult and drawn out, but you can help to simplify it by leaving an updated will that has been drawn up with professional help. If you have minor children, see that money is set aside for their well-being and specifically name a guardian who is to care for them if both parents should die; it does happen. Make sure in your will or in a special letter that you name those lawyers, bankers, and advisors who are aware of your affairs and who can help the executor sort through your business. I personally favor using a clause that stipulates that anyone contesting the will is automatically excluded from it. That often saves a lot of bickering.

There have been massive changes in trusts since 1976. If you have a will dated before 1977 that incorporates the use of a trust, it may need revision. I suggest you immediately contact your estate-planning attorney to update it and make the necessary changes.

Financial goals are personal and vary from one woman to another. Because they are so different, it would be impossible for me to do any more than suggest how you might achieve them, as I have tried to do throughout this book. The details of those plans are up to you, once you have assessed your own resources and talents and tastes. But if you've learned nothing else by now, you know that the possibilities truly are endless.

A final thought occurs to me; this question is asked at every lecture or seminar my company sponsors—"What percent of my net worth or investable monies should I place in the bank, stocks, real estate, commodities, or any other type of investment?" My reply is always the same, that there are no absolute ground rules. I have seen some advisors draw charts and graphs and even pyramids that indicate a certain percent should be allotted to high-risk, a certain percent to growth, and a certain percent to conservative investments.

Every woman will have a different degree of risk-taking

ability. I have a client in her sixties who loves the action of the commodity markets and is bored by utility stocks that might produce attractive dividends. I have another client with a substantial seven-figure net worth who would never consider anything riskier than a bond. I might add that the latter woman inherited the bulk of her money. We all are seeking to meet varying objectives, and we all have varying degrees of risk that we are willing to take to do so.

More and more, I am seeing both single and married women becoming actively involved in investments, overviews, objectives, and the everyday nuances of money.

Those of you who are fortunate enough to have substantial investable assets can select different opportunities that are attractive to you. Even if you have large sums available, you may choose to pool your dollars with others' simply as a means of diversifying and spreading the risk around.

Married (or living-together) couples often choose to keep their funds separate, allowing each individual to select his or her own investments. Couples sometimes even enjoy competing with each other to see how well they can do. More often than not in these situations, I have found that the woman surprises both herself and her partner as she sees how fast she is learning.

Take advantage of the numerous classes that are offered by various organizations and community colleges. If you feel a course is presenting too much data too quickly, don't hesitate to repeat it. I have had many clients do this and get more information each time. Often you just can't absorb it all at once; you need to let the new material sink in for a little while and then try again.

Your objectives and goals should become reachable for you. Do remember, though, that goals are rarely achieved overnight. It may sound incredibly old-hat, but patience is a virtue in money and investments. If you attempt too much too quickly and expect that everything you do will work perfectly the first time, you may be in for some disappointments and surprises.

Above all, keep working to reach your goal. As I have said earlier and as I have told class after class, you will certainly make mistakes, but by diversifying and always asking questions, you can learn to minimize your losses and maximize your capacity as an effective, informed investor.

11

WHEN AND HOW TO HIRE THE EXPERTS

A couple of facts ought to be obvious to you at this point as you contemplate your financial future. One, as I have just discussed, is that you will need a definite strategy to achieve whatever financial goal you set for yourself. Haphazard investments won't do it; you must coordinate your investments with the tax consequences of your income and the economic realities prevailing throughout the country. It is a difficult and demanding job that never ends. That brings up the second fact that should be self-evident: You can't do it all alone. You will have to rely on the help of specialists who know their way through the maze of laws and regulations and intricacies and refinements that are the mark of the present-day financial, legal, and tax worlds.

My purpose in this final chapter, now that I've exposed you to the various elements that may be part of your financial strategy, is to give you some criteria that you can use in choosing those specialists. I want to point you toward some of the sources of information you'll need in order to make intelligent financial decisions.

If you become even a semiserious investor, you will at one time or another deal with an accountant, a banker, a financial planner, a stock broker, a real estate broker, and a lawyer—or perhaps even several lawyers. The quality of the professionals in each of these areas varies greatly, and even among the competent and well qualified, there will be some who won't appeal to you simply because of their personality or demeanor.

As I mentioned earlier, I feel that all of us should have a yearly check-up with a financial planner, if merely to verify that we are on the right track. Most of us devote the majority of our time to making money, rather than putting together a strategy for how to manage and, we hope, increase it. On our own, we may not hear of new vehicles that can help. For example, T-bill accounts lasting only six months, Individual Retirement Accounts, and money market funds all were nonexistent ten years ago but today play an important role in financial planning.

When you don't know something, it's important to find out the answer from a pro and not a friend or a well-meaning amateur. Last year, I was addressing a group of women in one of our southern states. A woman asked me about the legal title on a certificate of deposit she had at the bank. She had her own money from a previous marriage and had remarried. At that time, the bank teller told her that she had to put both her new husband's name and her own on the certificate as owners. If the woman were to die unexpectedly, the teller informed her, it would make things easier if the certificate were held in joint ownership with her husband. I asked the woman whether she intended to give half the value of the certificate to her husband, and she said no, the money was to go to her daughter (from her first marriage) if she were to die. What I saw was a potentially very sticky situation, because if the woman did die, her husband might not want to give the money to his stepdaughter, and a gift tax should be declared.

This is a common example of advice that might be well intended but is not correct. A person who is a certified financial planner should be much more able to assist any woman with the nuances that should concern her in the everyday financial arena. New clients have rarely left my office after their first interview without several concepts that will benefit them personally.

My first bit of advice when you go out to find professional

assistance is to pay attention to the chemistry. There is no sense in dealing with someone, no matter how competent, who gives you a feeling of unease when you are working together.

To make that decision, of course, you first need a sample from which to choose. If you have no name with which to start, I suggest asking people similar to yourself, whose financial goals and abilities are about the same as your own. Ask them, too, whom they have dealt with in the past but have since left, and why. Your friends can do you a great favor by sharing their mistakes with you.

Attend financial seminars and discussions, but be aware that many of these are sponsored by investment firms as a means of recruiting new clients. Once your name has appeared on the list of those in attendance, the company will be calling you to give you a pitch. Despite that, and despite the fact that the information you get at these seminars might tend to be somewhat biased if they are sponsored by a single company, such meetings at least serve the dual function of bringing you together with people like yourself who are anxious to become serious investors and helping to acquaint you with the jargon and "buzz words" that are so dear to the hearts of professionals in any business. You'll be amazed at how simple some complicated explanations can be once you know the right words; that's why I've made an effort in this book to acquaint you with the vocabulary. Moreover, very often the instructors at these classes will be close to the local financial community.

If you attend a social gathering that includes business people in your community, listen to the conversation during dinner and don't, by any means, gravitate afterward to the room where the women have gathered. Instead, go off to wherever the men are talking. Probably they will be talking business, and I wouldn't be at all reticent about asking questions about the deals—what was the bank involved?—who did the accounting?—how was the deal structured?

Again, this will put you into contact with people from your area who are seriously interested in their own finances. You may be able to share experiences with one another.

If none of these channels is open to you, then you'll have to start with the basics. Read the business section of the local paper to see which lawyers and accountants and tax experts are mentioned most often. If necessary, start with the Yellow Pages of the telephone directory, going by trial and error until you find the people who suit you.

There are specific questions that you should ask the different professionals. In general, however, I would approach all of them by telephone, telling them that you are looking for assistance in their paricular field, and asking whether they would be willing to spend a few minutes with you. If they are, make an appointment. If not, cross them off your list. In the case of lawyers, accountants, and financial consultants, they ought to be willing to give you a few minutes without charge. This, however, does not entitle you to free advice on complicated legal and financial matters. The purpose of this free time is for you to acquaint yourself with them, and vice versa.

Remember in every case that the professional whom you're interviewing will be sizing you up as a potential client as well. This is probably desirable. In all likelihood, you don't belong with a professional who has so little business that he or she automatically takes on every would-be client who comes through the door.

Interview at least three accountants. Ask what their charges are; they could range from $50 to $100 an hour, and higher. The best firm for you is not necessarily the biggest in town. Smaller concerns, with just two or three principals in the office, could be very well suited to your needs. With large firms, in fact, you may be assigned an inexperienced junior member of the firm unless you have the clout to demand otherwise. Find out how long the accountant has been in business, and how long with the firm. Ask whether the firm uses computers, and the cost of that service to you.

Find out how clerical time in the office is billed (it shouldn't be as expensive as the accountant's time).

You should ask similar questions when speaking to lawyers. The services of a legal secretary shouldn't be billed at the same rate as those of the attorney. Ask about other charges, especially for telephone calls and photocopying, which can run surprisingly high. Just as important, find out whether the lawyer specializes, and in what area. You wouldn't want to consult a divorce attorney about a real estate problem. Since you may be dealing in several diverse areas, I would recommend against someone who works alone in an office. Far preferable is an attorney who is associated with other lawyers and so has access to specialists in many areas.

In life insurance, real estate, and the stock market, you will want to find somebody who has been in the business at least five years. The turnover in insurance sales representatives, real estate agents, and securities brokers is phenomenally high. When I worked for a stock brokerage house, my observation (later confirmed) was that 90 percent of trainees fail to last beyond the first year on the job. Of that remaining 10 percent, half quit the business before the end of the second year. This is understandable. Brokers don't get rich immediately—and often not at all. They are guaranteed a certain minimum salary for the first six months or year on the job, but they aren't likely to survive long if they don't quickly exceed that minimum with their commissions, which usually amount to about one-third of what you pay the brokerage house.

There are similar situations in insurance and real estate, with the added pitfall that those professions, especially real estate, are flooded with part-timers who have qualified for a license but haven't gotten into the business all the way.

In the chapter dealing with the stock market, I warned you about calling a brokerage house and asking to speak to a broker. The person who comes on the line at that point, the floor man or duty person, isn't necessarily the broker who can serve you best. Odds are that that person is a trainee who won't be around in six months or a year. So follow my advice in that chapter and contact the manager of a brokerage house and ask to be referred to a broker, not the floor person.

You can avoid the inexperienced amateurs in real estate and insurance by holding to two criteria: Avoid part-timers, who will do only a part-time job for you, and deal only with brokers and agents who have at least five years' experience. Anyone who has been able to survive for five years in either of those businesses, or the stock market, has probably got some special skills.

If you're the independent sort who likes to do your own research and evaluation with stocks, you might reduce your commissions by as much as 50 percent if you place your orders through a discount brokerage house. These firms advertise in the business sections of your local newspapers as well as in *The Wall Street Journal*.

A last note of admonition on the subject of stock brokers—be sure to ask whether the house is acting as investment broker (the firm that handles the actual process of bringing a stock to the public) for any stock in which you're interested. If so, you should know that because of legal restrictions, your broker in that firm probably will be the last to know the news, good or bad, that could affect the stock's performance. I worked for a brokerage house that acted as an investment broker for a large electronics company in the Palo Alto area. We kept up with news of that firm mostly by listening to rumors in other brokerage houses on the street.

When you interview financial planners and consultants, ask how the company charges—by fee, commission, or both—and the rates. Consulting fees, you'll recall, are tax deductible; commissions are not. Ask for the names of some clients whom you might contact for references. There is no ethical consideration that should prevent consultants from providing you with a few names. If one refuses, drop him or her and go on to another. Ask about office hours—will they be available when you are free, or will you have to conform to their schedule?—and ask what kind of continuing education the members of the firm are required to undergo. This is important, because laws and practices change quickly. You might ask the representative of the firm with whom you speak how many clients with gross earnings of $50,000 a year pay federal taxes in the $12,000 area when filing jointly. (Single taxpayers might raise the figure to $15,000.) The answer should be "Few." If it's not, then that company may be neglecting its clients' tax problems.

I have already mentioned some of the sources of information that may help you deal better with the stock market. *The Wall Street Journal, Forbes, Barron's, Business Week, Fortune, Money,* the *Value Line Survey,* and the *Kiplinger Letter* are just a few. All contain facts and analyses that may help you to execute your financial plan. I might add to that list a free publication, the monthly newsletter of the Federal Reserve, which is sent without charge upon request. Addresses for the above-mentioned publications can be found in Appendix II.

One TV program that deals intelligently with financial matters, especially the stock market, is the Public Broadcasting System's weekly production, "Wall Street Week," hosted by Louis Rukeyser.

Still, the truth is that you can swamp yourself with information and read so many books and newspapers and magazines and stock guides that you have no time at all for investing. You must be selective, and to do that you have to know what to reject because it is of no use to you and what to absorb because it deals with a subject that is close to you. That, in turn, implies that you have some sort of coherent, consistent financial plan, that you have picked out a goal and have chosen the means by which you will achieve that goal.

This plan, which I keep coming back to, is a vehicle for making the materials that you care for, whatever they may be, more abundant in your life. The strategy you choose will be a part of your life, and, as such, it will be affected by, and ought to include, life's upsets and catastrophes. Moreover, the strategy will require a good deal of time and hard work and energy. The rewards are immense, though; they can give you the kind of freedom and security that is fast becoming every woman's birthright.

NET WORTH STATEMENT FORM

Assets

1. Checking Accounts

   Bank: _____   Amount _____
   Bank: _____   Amount _____
   (should only contain one month's expenses)

   _____

2. Savings Accounts—Passbook
   Savings and Loan_____   Amount_____
   Savings and Loan_____   Amount_____
   Savings and Loan_____   Amount_____

   _____

3. Certificates of Deposit

	Rate	Matures	Amount
Bank or Savings and Loan	____	____	____
Bank or Savings and Loan	____	____	____
Bank or Savings and Loan	____	____	____
Bank or Savings and Loan	____	____	____

   _____

4. Money Market Funds

   Company _____   Amount _____
   Company _____   Amount _____

   _____

5. Credit Union

   _____

6. Government

	Rate	Matures	Amount
Treasury Bills	____	_____	_____
Treasury Bonds	____	_____	_____
Treasury Notes	____	_____	_____

_____

7. Bonds—Municipal and Corporate

Company or Municipality	Number of Bonds	Rate	Maturity	Original Cost	Market Value
_____	_____	_____	_____	_____	_____
_____	_____	_____	_____	_____	_____
_____	_____	_____	_____	_____	_____
_____	_____	_____	_____	_____	_____

_____

8. Life Insurance—Cash Value

Company	Amount of Insurance	Cash Value
_____	_____	_____
_____	_____	_____
_____	_____	_____

_____

9. Annuities

	Rate	Amount
Company _____	_____	_____
Company _____	_____	_____

_____

10. Stocks

Number of Shares	Company	Purchase Date	Original Cost	Dividends	Current Market Value
_____	_____	_____	_____	_____	_____
_____	_____	_____	_____	_____	_____
_____	_____	_____	_____	_____	_____
_____	_____	_____	_____	_____	_____

_____

11. Stock—Privately Held Companies—Nonliquid   _____

12. Mutual Funds

Number of shares	Company	Pur-chase Date	Original Cost	Current Market
_____	_____	____	_____	_____
_____	_____	____	_____	_____

13. Real Estate
     Residence   _____
     Second or Vacation Home   _____
     Income Property   _____
         Apartments _____

     Commercial
     Buildings _____

     Shopping
     Center _____

14. Limited Partnership   _____
     Public
     Company _____   Purchase Amount _____
     Company _____   Purchase Amount _____
     Private
     Type _____   Purchase Amount _____
     Type _____   Purchase Amount _____

15. Commodities
     Individual Contracts   _____
     Managed Accounts   _____

16. Art   _____
17. Jewelry   _____
18. Coins   _____
19. Antiques   _____

20. Personal Items
    Automobiles   _____
    Furniture   _____
    Other   _____

                                              _____

21. Other Assets of Value   _____

Liabilities

1. Mortgages
   Residence   _____
   Second   or   Vacation
   House   _____
   Income Property   _____
                                   _____

                                              _____

2. Commercial Loans
   Automobile   _____
   Unsecured   _____
   Secured   _____

                                              _____

3. Personal Debts
   Furniture   _____
   IOU's
   Mastercharge   _____
   VISA   _____
   Medical Bills   _____
   Credit Cards   _____
                                   _____
                                   _____
                                   _____

                                              _____

To calculate net worth, add up all assets and all liabilities.
Subtract the liabilities from the assets. You should have a
surplus of assets, the larger the better. If you don't, run—
don't walk—for help and stop using your charge cards.

Appendix II

(Sources of Information)

GOVERNMENT AGENCIES
If you have a question regarding the Truth in Lending Act or about discrimination in lending:
    For national banks, write:

    Office of Consumer Affairs
    Controller of the Currency
    490 L'Enfant Plaza, S.W.
    Washington, D.C. 20219
For state-chartered banks that are members of the Federal Reserve System, write:

    Division of Consumer Affairs
    Federal Reserve System
    21st St. & Constitution Ave., N.W.
    Washington, D.C. 20551

or the appropriate regional branch:

    33 Liberty St.
    New York, N.Y. 10045

    30 Pearl St.
    Boston, Massachusetts 02110

    411 Locust St.
    St. Louis, Missouri 63166

    250 Marquette Ave.
    Minneapolis, Minnesota 55480

1455 East Sixth St.
Cleveland, Ohio 44101

925 Grand Ave.
Kansas City, Missouri 64198

400 Sansome St.
San Francisco, California 94120

230 S. LaSalle
Chicago, Illinois 60690

400 S. Akard St.
Dallas, Texas 75222

925 Chestnut St.
Philadelphia, Pennsylvania 19105

104 Marietta St., N.W.
Atlanta, Georgia 30303

100 N. Ninth St.
Richmond, Virginia 23261

In reference to savings and loans, both federally-chartered and state-chartered, that are insured by the Federal Savings and Loans Corporation, write:

Office of the Secretary
Federal Home Loan Bank Board
320 First St., N.W.
Washington, D.C. 20552

For Federally-chartered credit unions:

Office of the Administrator
National Credit Union Administration
2025 M St., N.W.
Washington, D.C. 20456

For information regarding land development:

    Office of Interstate Land Sales Registration
    U.S. Department of Housing and Urban Development
    451 Seventh St., S.W.
    Washington, D.C. 20410

For securities problems, including stocks, bonds, options, limited partnerships:

    Office of Consumer Affairs
    Securities and Exchange Commission
    500 N. Capital St., N.W.
    Washington, D.C. 20549

    Surveillance Department
    National Association of Securities Dealers
    1735 K St., N.W.
    Washington, D.C. 20006

or the Corporations Commissioner of the appropriate state.

INFORMATION ON STOCKS AND BONDS

Value Line Survey
Arnold Bernhard & Co., Inc.
711 Third Ave.
New York, N.Y. 10017
Approximate cost: $283/year

Standard & Poor's Stock Reports
25 Broadway
New York, N.Y. 10004
N.Y. Cost: $425/year
American: $350/year
Over the Counter: $350/year

Standard and Poor's Stock Guide (Indiv.)
same address as above
$52/year

Standard and Poor's Bond Guide (Indiv.)
$85/year

How to Buy Stocks, sixth rev. ed.
Engel, Louis & Wycoff, Peter
New York: Bantam Books, 1977
$2.95

INFORMATION ON MUTUAL FUNDS

Wiesenberger Investment Companies Services
870 7th Ave.
New York, N.Y. 10019
$34/year

The above-mentioned references are available at brokerage firms
and most public libraries.

MONEY MARKET FUNDS

There are numerous funds available, of which a few are listed
below. In addition, several brokerage firms have their own money
funds for clients.

Dreyfus Liquid Assets
The Bank of New York
Dreyfus Service Corporation
P.O. Box 12139
Newark, New Jersey 07101

Oppenheimer Monetary Bridge Fund
One New York Plaza
New York, N.Y. 10004

Reserve Fund
810 Seventh Ave.
New York, N.Y. 10019

Capital Preservation
755 Page Mill Road
Palo Alto, California 94304

Kemper Money Market Fund
120 South La Salle St.
Chicago, Illlinois 60603

PUBLICATIONS

The Kiplinger Washington Letter
1729 H St., N.W.
Washington, D.C. 20006
$42/year; weekly publication

"Monetary Trends"
Federal Reserve Bank of St. Louis
P. O. Box 442
St. Louis, Missouri 63166
Free; monthly publication

Money Magazine
% Time, Inc.
541 No. Fairbanks Ct.
Chicago, Illinois 60611
$19.95/year; weekly publication

Business Week
425 Battery St.
San Francisco, California 94111
$31/year; weekly publication

Forbes
60 Fifth Ave.
New York, N.Y. 10011
$27/year; weekly publication

Fortune
% Time, Inc.
541 No. Fairbanks Ct.
Chicago, Illinois 60611
$32/year; weekly publication

The Wall Street Journal
$56/year; daily publication, check with local distributor to subscribe

Barron's Magazine
200 Barrett Rd.
Chicopee, Massachusetts 01021
$12/year; weekly publication

INVESTMENT LETTERS

There are numerous advisory letters available to the general public. It is recommended that you check your local newspapers and *The Wall Street Journal* for advertisements relating to complimentary copies and/or seek recommendations from professional investors who take various advisory letters as to which might be suitable to you.

GLOSSARY OF
BUSINESS TERMS

Annuity: A contract that is issued by a life insurance company for a given amount of money and guarantees a return of regular income for the rest of the annuitant's life or possibly, depending on the way the contract is written, longer. For example, if the holder of a "ten years certain" policy were to die before the ten years were up, her beneficiary would receive an annual income for the remainder of that period.

Assets: Everything that a corporation, partnership, or individual holds or has due to it. For example, cash, investments, accounts receivable, raw materials, and inventory are all current assets, while such things as patents and good will are intangible assets.

Bear Market: The stock market when it is in a decline. The person known as a bear is one who believes the market will decline.

Bearer Bond: A bond that does not have the owner's name registered on its face or on the books of the issuing company. (Because the owner's name is not registered, these bonds are especially vulnerable to theft and should be kept in a safe place.)

Book Value: An accounting term for stock, the number that results from taking all the assets—current, fixed, and intangible—of a corporation, subtracting all its debts and other obligations, and finally dividing by the number of common shares outstanding.

Bond: Basically an IOU from a corporation or municipality, a bond represents a loan, and the holder of the bond is a creditor. (Note: the holder does not act as a shareholder of the corporation.) The corporation or municipality agrees to pay the holder a guaranteed rate of interest for a specific term. Sometimes bonds are secured, or backed by collateral (for example, a particular model of aircraft could serve as collateral for a bond issued by an airplane company), and sometimes not, in which case they are issued on the good faith and general reliability of the corporation or municipality. In addition, corporate bonds can be *convertible* or *non-convertible;* if convertible, a bond can be exchanged for a pre-determined amount of the corporation's common stock.

Broker: An agent who handles buy and sell orders for the public in securities and commodities and receives a commission for his or her services in those transactions.

Bull Market: A market that is appreciating. A bull is someone who feels the market will go up in value.

Call Option: The right (which itself is bought and sold) to buy a specific number of shares of a specific stock at a specific price for a specified period of time. The investor who purchases a call hopes and anticipates that the underlying stock price will increase. The amount of the contract the purchaser pays is called a premium. A stock is said to be *called away* when the purchaser of the call option requires the seller to deliver the underlying stock.

Capitalization: The total value (usually the *par,* or stated, value at the time of issuance) of all securities that are issued by a corporation, including bonds and preferred and common stock.

Certificate of Deposit (also known as a *CD):* An instrument, usually issued in $1,000 denominations, that represents savings deposited in a bank or savings and loan institution for a specified period of time. For example, a depositor leaves $1,000 with a bank and receives a certificate guaranteeing 7¾ percent interest for six years as opposed to the approximate rate of 5½ percent that a passbook account would offer. If the depositor should withdraw her savings before the CD matures, she would be faced with a substantial penalty against the interest that has been accruing.

Commercial Paper: Promissory notes for loans made to corporations. The amounts are usually large, the interest rates high, and the terms short (ranging from overnight to several months or more).

Commodities Contract: An agreement that allows the bearer to purchase a specified quantity of foodstuffs, fibers, currency, wood, metals, or other materials at a specified time and price. There are approximately a dozen commodity exchanges in the United States; the biggest of these is the Chicago Board of Trade.

Compound Interest: Interest paid on accumulated interest as well as on the principal sum invested.

Consolidation Loan: A loan that is taken out to pay off numerous smaller debts and consolidate all the payments into one. Such loans are usually offered by finance companies (as opposed to banks) at extremely high rates of interest.

Coupon: The part of a bearer bond that represents the payable interest. The bond holder merely clips the coupon and takes it to a bank for collection. If a brokerage firm holds the bond, it will clip the coupon and credit your account with the interest.

Day Order: An order to buy or sell stock that expires at the end of the trading day if it is not executed on that day.

Deferred Annuity: An annuity that provides for the income payments to start at a future date and therefore accumulates interest during the deferral period. A deferred annuity often begins with a lump sum and receives tax-favored status on withdrawal.

Depreciation: A bookkeeping entry that represents no cash outlay and enables the owner of a building, for example, to deduct part of its original cost over the building's useful life. If the building is worth $20,000 and its useful life is twenty years, twenty would be divided into $20,000 and the owner would write off (depreciate) $1,000 a year.

Dividend: A payment distributed to shareholders of a corporation on a pro rata basis. On preferred stock it is a fixed amount; on common stock the dividend may vary and may be eliminated by the board of directors if the business is not doing well. Often a company will issue a stock dividend in lieu of a cash dividend to avoid depleting cash reserves.

Doomsday Investments: Investments in areas (for example, gold, silver, and collectibles) that traditionally perform contrary to th

stock market; such investments are particularly popular in inflationary or unstable times.

Earnings Report: An income statement that is issued by a company, showing its earnings or losses for a specific period. It indicates the source of revenues and expenses and the net profit or loss.

Ex-Dividend: Without dividend. A stock that has declared a dividend will pay that dividend to the shareholders, both old and new, up to a specific date. After that date, the stock is then "ex." Anyone who purchases that stock on or after the ex-dividend date must wait for the next declarable date in order to participate in dividends.

Exercise an Option: Indicates that the holder of the option has chosen to have the underlying stock delivered to her at the *exercise price* (the price for that stock that is specified in the option).

FIFO: In annuities, stands for "First in, first out" and is an accounting method based on an IRS policy that specifies that early withdrawals of revenue from the annuity, up to the original amount of the annuity, are considered to come from that initial sum and are not taxable.

Float: The amount of stock that is traded of a given company. A company with a *thin* float has few shares that are traded or available for purchase on an open basis.

"Flower Bonds": Certain Treasury bonds that mature immediately upon the death of the person in whose name they are issued. Said to be as "common as flowers" at the deathbeds of the well-to-do, they are sometimes bought in the name of someone who is terminally ill so that their increased value can be used to help pay estate taxes.

General Partner: The person (or persons) who manages a limited partnership in exchange for compensation, usually in the form of a percentage of revenues and/or of the profits upon sale. The general partner is responsible and liable for all operational decisions affecting the partnership.

Good Till Cancelled Order (GTC Order), or *Open Order:* Unlike a

day order, an order to buy or sell stock that remains in effect until the broker executes it or the client withdraws it.

Holding Company: A corporation that owns the securities of another company or corporation and, in most cases, has voting control over it.

Hypothecation: Putting up securities as collateral for a loan. Hypothecation is quite often done in cases of *margin buying*—when the purchaser uses her stock holdings to secure a loan that will enable her to buy other stocks.

Inactive Stock: Usually a stock that is trading on an exchange or over the counter at a rate of only a few hundred shares a day. This is also known as *thin stock*.

Investment Company: Also known as a mutual fund, a company or trust that invests its capital in other companies. There are two types of investment companies, *closed-end* and *open-end*. Closed-end funds have limited number of shares outstanding and are traded as a stock normally would be, on the New York or American Stock Exchanges or the over-the-counter market. Open-end funds, which can continue to issue more shares as the demand for them increases, sell their own shares directly to investors and stand ready to buy them back. Funds may also be *load* or *no-load*, depending on whether or not they carry a commission charge.

Investment Tax Credit (ITC): A credit granted by the IRS on a capital item that has a useful life of several years. At present, a full 10 percent of the original cost will be granted for an item with a useful life of seven years; 6⅔ percent for one with a useful life of five years, and 3⅓ percent for one with a useful life of three years. The ITC is taken the year the item is purchased.

IRA (Individual Retirement Account): A program that allows an individual employee who is not covered by a pension or profit-sharing program to place up to 15 percent of her income or $1500, whichever is less, in a tax-deferred retirement plan every year. The money may be invested in specified forms of real estate, stocks, mutual funds, bank accounts, insurance policies, savings and loans, and other approved plans.

Joint Venture: An investment project in which two or more

partners share all profits and liabilities in accordance with their share of the original investment.

Keogh Plan: A retirement plan that allows a self-employed individual to place $7500 or 15 percent of her income, whichever is less, in a tax-deferred retirement program similar to an *IRA*.

Leverage: The borrowing of money to finance a portion of an investment. For example, if you purchase a property for $10,000 and put down $2,000, borrowing $8,000 at 12 percent, and sell the property three years later for $15,000, you will have received a $5,000 gain minus the cost of the loan at 12 percent for ten years (approximately $2,800), netting you $2,200, or a little over 100 percent. If you pay all cash for the land, you will reap a $5,000 profit—a return on your investment of only 50 percent.

Liabilities: All claims against a corporation, entity, or individual, including accounts, salaries, and dividends payable, accrued taxes, and any debts such as bank loans or outstanding bonds.

Limit Order: An order directing a broker to buy or sell stock at a specific price.

Limited Partnership: A pooling of funds for investment purposes that allows the investor to take a passive role while a general partner manages the investment. The limited partner's liability is usually confined to her original investment; she does not have management responsibilities or participate in day-to-day decisions.

Liquid Assets: Investments or assets that can be turned into cash within a very short period of time, for example, passbook savings accounts, money market funds, certificates of deposit, and selected deferred annuities. Some cash investments, such as annuities and certificates of deposit, may have penalties and/or reduction of interest for early withdrawal of funds.

Load: A sales commission that is included as a portion of the offering price of shares of a mutual fund. The load is incurred at the time of purchase, and there are usually no additional charges or commissions when the investor sells. A *no-load* mutual fund is one that does not charge this commission.

Long-Term Losses and Gains: For tax purposes, a profit or loss that results from any investment that is held for one year or longer.

Long-term losses and gains are taxed at a lower rate than the investor's usual tax rate.

Margin Buying: A method for purchasing stock through a brokerage firm by borrowing money or obtaining credit from the broker. Currently, an investor must put up 50 percent of the purchase price, with a minimum deposit of $2,000.

Margin Call: A demand that the investor put up additional money or securities with the broker. This happens either when a new purchase is made or when the customer's total equity in the margin account declines below a specific minimum that is set by the New York Stock Exchange and/or brokerage house.

Market Order: An order directing a broker to buy or sell a specific number of shares of a stock at the most advantageous price that can be obtained when the order is originally placed.

Market Price: The most recent reported price at which a security was sold.

Maturity: The date on which a loan or a bond becomes due and payable to the bond holder.

Money Market Certificates: Instruments that banks and savings and loan institutions offer to their savers, usually in minimums of $10,000, allowing savers to participate in the current Treasury bill rates. Money market certificates usually earn more than passbook savings or certificate of deposit rates with a commitment of funds for six months.

Money Market Funds: A form of investment company (mutual fund) in which the assets are invested in money instruments such as government bonds, notes, Treasury bills, Certificates of Deposit of large banks, commercial paper, and banker's acceptances. Money market funds usually have minimum amounts required to join them—for example, $1,000 versus the larger amount required for money market certificates—and are offered by institutions other than banks and savings and loans. Interest is earned daily, checkwriting privileges are often offered (usually for a minimum of $500), and one is usually entitled to make additional deposits in minimums of $100.

Mutual Fund: See *Investment Company.*

Net Asset Value: For investment companies, the total market value of all the shares that are owned minus liabilities, if any, divided by the number of outstanding shares. The resulting figure, the net asset value, is listed in the newspapers each day.

Net Worth: For an individual or a corporation, all of the assets minus all of the liabilities.

Odd Lot: A quantity of stock, or number of shares, that is smaller than the standard trading unit (usually 100 shares).

Option: In the stock market, a contract that gives the bearer the right to purchase or sell a specific stock at a specific price within a specific period of time. (See also *Call Option* and *Put Option.*)

Ordinary Life Insurance: See *Straight Life Insurance*.

Paper Profit: Unrealized profit on a security or investment still held. Paper profits become actual profits only when the holdings are sold.

Par Value: For bonds, the amount that appears on the face of the bond and is payable at maturity. For stocks, a dollar amount assigned by a corporation's charter to each share of stock. Par value today has little meaning to buyers of common stock and has no relationship at all to the market or book value. For preferred stock, par value does have meaning because it is often the basis on which dividends are calculated.

Points: The interest rate charged by a lending institution. One point would be one percent, three points three percent. If you borrowed $10,000 at a charge of one point, the fee would be $100.

Price-Earnings (P-E) Ratio: The price of a share of stock divided by its earnings for the past year. A stock that has been earning $3 per share and selling for $18 per share is said to be trading at a price-earnings ratio of six to one.

Private Partnership: An investment partnership in which there are fewer than thirty-five partners, each of whom is required to have met certain standards that are stated in the partnership agreement.

Probate: The process whereby the executor of an estate presents a will to the court to have it declared valid.

Proxy: A written authorization given by a shareholder to enable someone else to represent her and vote her shares at a shareholders' meeting.

Public Partnership: A limited partnership in which thirty-five investors or more (often into the thousands) pool their funds for investment purposes. Like all limited partnerships, public partnerships have a general partner who makes day-to-day management decisions.

Quotation: Often called a *quote*, the highest price at which anyone is willing to buy and the lowest price at which anyone is willing to sell a security in the stock market at a given time.

Rally: A quick rise following a decline in the price level of an individual stock or the market in general.

Refinancing: Taking on a new debt to cancel out an old one. In the case of securities, this means that the issuing company sells new securities and uses the money to retire outstanding securities or debts. In the case of a real estate, it involves taking out a new mortgage so that the old one may be paid off, possibly leaving the property owner with additional capital that may be used as she chooses.

Registered Bond: In contrast to a *bearer bond,* a bond that is listed in the owner's name on the books of the issuing company.

REIT (Real Estate Investment Trust): An organization that is very similar to an investment company but concentrates its holdings in real estate. The yield is often substantial, as REITs are required to distribute up to 90 percent of their income to investors.

Roll-over: A tax-free transfer of funds—for example, taking a lump sum beyond payment received from a pension or profit-sharing program when you leave a job and moving it, or "rolling it over," to an *IRA*.

Round Lot: The standard unit in which securities are traded. On the exchanges the unit of trading is usually 100 shares for stock and $1,000 par value for bonds.

Second Trust Deed: A method of lending money to an individual with a parcel of real estate used as collateral. These investments pay higher than normal bank rates of interest and are considered non-liquid, usually lasting from six months to three years.

Securities: A broad term that covers stocks, bonds, partnership investments, and any other investment that can be purchased through a broker.

Short Selling: A method of selling stocks that you do not own by borrowing the shares through a broker. If your stock declines in value, you purchase it back at the lower figure and declare the gain. On the other hand, if the stock appreciates in value, you will show a loss when you buy it back. This is a highly speculative move that can have unlimited liabilities if the stock increases in market value.

Short-Term Losses and Gains: Under IRS regulations, any profit or loss that results from securities or investments held for less than a year. Short-term losses and gains are taxable at the individual or corporation's normal tax rate.

Split: The division of the outstanding shares of stock in a corporation into more shares. For example, in a two-for-one split, a company with 1,000,000 shares outstanding would have 2,000,000 outstanding after the split. In a *reverse split,* the same company would declare a one-for-two split, leaving it with 500,000 shares outstanding. A company will often split its stock so that it can sell shares at a lower (and therefore more commercially attractive) price.

Stock: Partial ownership in a corporation as represented by negotiable shares. There are two kinds of stock, *common* and *preferred;* common stock has no fixed, guaranteed dividend, while preferred stock will pay a specified dividend as long as the company is solvent.

Stock Dividend: A dividend that is paid in securities rather than in cash. The dividend will be for additional shares of the issuing company or of a subsidiary.

Straight Life Insurance (also called *Ordinary Life* or *Whole-Life Insurance*): Often referred to as an insurance policy with a bank account since the policy's cash value increases from year to year. Straight life insurance costs considerably more than *term insurance* in the early years of ownership, but premiums remain constant from that point on.

Strike Price: The price at which you may purchase the underlying shares of an option. For example, if you buy one call of XYZ Corporation at thirty dollars per share, the strike price is thirty dollars per share.

Tax Bracket: Not the average percentage of your income payable in taxes, but the percentage of any new income (above what you are currently making) that would have to be earmarked for taxes. For example, if you are married and have a taxable income of approximately $45,000, you will be in the 50 percent tax bracket— meaning that everything you earn over $45,000, until the next level, will be taxed at 50 percent.

Tax-Exempt Bond: Another name for a *municipal bond* (that is, one issued by a state or local government) because the interest is exempt from both state and federal taxes.

Tender: An offer from one company to buy all or part of the outstanding shares of another company for a stated price. The management of the sought-after company may accept or reject the tender; if it does reject the offer, it will advise its shareholders via public advertisements and letters to refuse to sell.

Term Insurance: Pure life insurance, without a savings policy, that gives you a specified amount of protection for a specified period of time, or term. The shorter the period of coverage and the younger you are, the lower the yearly premium.

Treasury Bills: U.S. Government obligations that are issued at auction for a minimum of $10,000. Their maturity date is a year or less from the date of issue and represents current interest rates. Proceeds from Treasury bills are used to finance the day-to-day operations of the government.

Treasury Bonds: Government instruments that mature a minimum of five years from the date of issue, unless (see *"flower bonds"*) the person in whose name they are issued dies.

Treasury Notes: Government obligations, similar to T-bills and T-notes, that mature within five years of issuance.

Trust: A legal instrument in which property or money is set aside to be managed by a trustee on behalf of a beneficiary. If properly executed, trusts can often save substantial tax dollars upon the death of the participants.

Unlisted (also known as *Over-the-Counter*) *Stock:* A security that is not traded on a stock exchange. When a company goes public by selling shares, its securities will trade on the over-the-counter market. At a later date the company will decide whether to continue trading over the counter or to apply to one of the major exchanges.

Whole-Life Insurance: See *Straight Life Insurance.*

Wrap-Around Mortgage (also known as a *Uniform Real Estate Contract,* a *Land Sales Contract,* or *Seller Carries the Financing*): A method of financing a real estate purchase in which the seller receives monthly payments from the new buyer and uses part of those payments to make the payments on the already existing loan—keeping the difference as reimbursement for the portion of the equity that was not covered by the new buyer's down payment. For example, if you made a down payment of $20,000 on a $100,000 house on which there was an existing loan of $50,000, the seller would be financing a total of $80,000. Assuming a 10 percent interest rate, you would pay the seller $800 per month, out of which she would pay $500 toward the existing mortgage and keep the remaining $300 for herself.

Yield (also known as *Return*): Dividends or interest paid by a company expressed as a percentage of the current price. For example, a stock with a current market value of forty dollars per share that pays dividends at two dollars per share is said to return 5 percent ($2 divided by $40). The return on a bond is calculated the same way: An 8 percent, $1,000 bond that sells at a discount for $800 has a current yield of 10 percent ($80 divided by $800).

Yield to Maturity: The yield of a bond at maturity, taking into account the price discount or premium over the face amount. If the price is greater than the stated face value, the bond is selling at a premium; if it is less, the bond is selling at a discount.

INDEX

Accountants, 186–87
Acquisitions, 93–96
Alimony, deduction for, 35–36
American Stock Exchange
    (AMEX), 88, 89
Annual reports, 92, 93
Annuities, 66–71
    life only, 70
    ten-year certain, 70–71
    twenty-year certain, 71
Apartment buildings, 139,
    144–46
Automobile, deduction for, 33–34
Avon company, 93–94

Balance sheet
    choosing a stock and, 123
    net worth, 14–19
Bally Manufacturing, 101
Bankruptcy, stockholders, 124–25
Bay Area Rapid Transit (BART)
    Authority, bonds issued by,
    106–7
Bonds, 103–7
    collateralized, 103
    convertible, 104
    corporate, 15, 49, 103–6
    government, 15
    municipal, 15, 49, 106–7
    treasury, 61
Brokerage houses, 187–88

Brokers, 126–29
Building permit, 141
Business expenses, deduction for,
    34–35

Calls, 108–11
Certificates of deposit, 14–15, 49,
    59–60
Checking accounts, 14–15
Chicago Board of Options, 112
Child care credits, 36
Clubs, 35
Coins, gold, 54
Collectibles, 16, 53–56
Commercial paper, 61–62
Commodities (commodities
    contracts), 118–21
    for gold, 55
    for silver, 55
Common stock, 102
Community property, 174
Community property laws,
    reform of, 80
Consolidation loans, 82
Consultants, 188–89
Convertible bonds, 104
Corporate bonds, 15, 49, 103–6
Corporations, 151–52
Credit, 72–84
    complaints concerning, 83–84
    See also Leverage; Loans

Credit cards, float and, 78–80
Credit rating, 10
Credit report, 10–14, 82
Credit unions, 60, 81

Death of a spouse, 4
    financial planning and, 174–80
Deductions, *see* Tax deductions
Dental expenses, deduction for,
    34
Diamonds, 55
Disney, Walt, 90
Dividends, 91
    choosing a stock and, 123
Divorce, 172–74
Doomsday investments, 53
Down payments on real estate,
    146–48

Earnings, choosing a stock and,
    123
Educational expenses, deduction
    for, 37
Emergency fund, 31
Equal Credit Opportunity Act,
    80–82, 83–84
Estate planning, treasury bonds
    in, 61
Exemptions on W-4 form, 26–27
Exercise price, 108
Experts, 183–90
    accountants, 186–87
    brokers, 187–88
    financial planners, 184, 188–89
    lawyers, 187
Exploratory oil and gas
    partnerships, 152–53

Fair Credit Reporting Act, 11
Federal Deposit Insurance
    Corporation (FDIC), 63

FIFO (First In, First Out) policy,
    annuities and, 67, 70
Finance companies, 82
Financial plan, 169–82
    death of a spouse and, 174–80
    divorce and, 172–74
    goals and, 180–82
    probate and, 180
Financial planners, 188–89
Float, 77–80

Gambling and entertainment
    businesses, stocks in, 100–1
Gemstones, 55
Goals, long-range, 9–10, 180–82
Gold, 53–55
Government bonds, 15

Health insurance premiums,
    deduction for, 34
Home office, deduction for, 36
Houses, margin buying and,
    114–15

Income tax, *see* Taxes
Individual Retirement Account
    (IRA), 40–42
Inflation, 45–56
    borrowing during periods of,
    46–48
    causes of, 46
    hedges against, 49
    second trust deeds and, 65
Insurance, life, *see* Life insurance
Interest, deduction for, 34
Internal Revenue Service (IRS),
    refund checks from, 25
Investment advisory fees,
    deduction for, 35
Investment tax credit, 36
    tax shelters and, 43

IOUs, 66

Joint ventures, 149–50

Keogh plan, 41–42
K-1 forms, 157

Land, unimproved, 140–42, 147
Lawyers, 187
Legal fees, deduction for, 35
Leveraging, 53, 72–79
Life insurance, 175–80
  cash value of, 63–64
  term, 176–78
  whole-life, 177–78
Limited partnership, 16, 150–68
  agricultural, 154
  corporations distinguished
    from, 151–52
  disclosure rules for, 154–58
  general partner in, 150–51
  oil and gas, 152–53
  prospectus of, 155–58, 167
  real estate, 31, 153–54, 158–66
Limit order, 128
Living-together arrangements,
    171–72
Loans, 79–84
  consolidation, 82
  Equal Credit Opportunity Act
    and, 80
  from finance companies, 82
  shopping around for, 81
Losses
  net operating, 38–39
  long-term, 39

Management firms for rental
    housing, 136
Margin buying, 114–15

Marital status, financial planning
    and, 169–73, 181
Market order, 127
Medical expenses, deduction for,
    34
Mergers, 93–96
Merrill Lynch, 87
Mobile homes, 137–38
Money market certificates, 63
Money market funds, 61–63
Mortgages, 146–48
Multi-unit homes, 138–39,
    143–44
Municipal bonds, 15, 49, 106–7
Mutual funds, 61, 115–18
  closed-ended and open-ended,
    116
  load and no-load, 116–17

National Association of
    Investment Clubs, 87
Net operating losses, 38–39
Net worth, determining your
    own, 11–19
New York Stock Exchange
    (NYSE), 85, 88, 89
NOW (Negotiable Order of
    Withdrawal) accounts, 58

Odd lots, 115
Office buildings, 139–40
Oil and gas partnerships, 152–53
Oil and gas program,
    developmental-exploratory,
    31
Oil and gas shelters, 43
Options, 107–12
  exercising the, 108, 110
Organizations, 35
Over-the-counter market, 89

Paintings, 56
Partnerships, limited, *see*
    Limited partnership
Passbook accounts, *see* Savings
    accounts
Personal property, 17
Planning, *see* Financial plan
Political contributions, 36
Preferred stock, 102–3
Price-earnings ratio, choosing a
    stock and, 123
Private offerings, 167
Probate, 174, 180
Professionals, *see* Experts
Prospectus for partnerships,
    155–58, 167
Public offerings, 167
Puts, 108, 111–12

Quarterly reports, 92, 93

Real estate, 131–48
    apartment buildings, 139,
        144–46
    commercial complexes, 139–40
    down payments, 146–48
    evaluating a property, 143–46
    inflation and, 50, 51, 53
    multi-unit homes, 138–39,
        143–44
    on net worth balance sheet,
        15–17
    popularity of, 131–32
    raw land, 140–42, 147
    renovations, 142–43
    single-family homes, 133–38
Real estate partnerships, 153–54,
    158–66
Recession, 46
Refinancing your house, 30
Renovations, 142–43

Research and development
    program, 31
Resorts International, 100
Retirement programs, 40–42
Rukeyser, Louis, 189

Sales tax, 34
Savings account (passbook
    accounts), 14, 31, 58
    annuities compared to, 67–70
    in credit unions, 60
    inflation and, 49
Second trust deeds, 64–66
Securities Exchange Commission,
    93, 154
Selling short, 112–13
Semiconductor companies, 101–2
Shopping malls, 139–40
Shorting, 112–13
Silver, 55
Single-family homes, 133–38
Specialists, *see* Experts
Stamps, 55–56
Standard and Poor's (S&P) index
    of stocks, 98–99
State tax, 34
Stock, 49–50, 90–103, 121–30
    acquisitions and mergers and,
        93–96
    bankruptcy of company and,
        124–25
    choosing, 121–24
    common, 102
    company purchase of their
        own, 92–93
    in gambling and entertainment
        businesses, 100–1
    information on, 125–26
    margin buying, 114–15
    of mutual funds, 115–18
    on net worth balance sheet, 15
    in odd lots, 115

option market for, 107–12
over-the-counter market for, 89
placing an order for, 126–29
preferred, 102–3
selling short, 112–13
in semiconductor companies, 101–2
Stockholders, rights of, 91–92
Stockholders' meetings, 92, 93
Stock market, 85–89
information on, 125–26
Stock quotations, 96
Stock-sharing plans, 90–91
Stop limit order, 128
Strike price, 108

Tax Act of 1976, 35
Tax brackets, 22–25
Tax credits
for alternative energy devices, 37
investment, see Investment tax credit
Tax deductions, 26–27, 32–40
for alimony, 35–36
for automobile expenses, 33–34
for business expenses, 34–35
children and, 36–37
for donations of clothing, 34
for educational expenses, 37
for health insurance premiums, 34
for home office, 37
for interest on loans, 34
for investment advisory fees, 35
for legal fees, 35
for medical and dental expenses, 34
for newspapers and magazines, 37

recordkeeping and, 33
for retirement programs, 40–42
for state tax and sales tax, 34
for stock market losses, 35
for visits to vacation-rental property, 35
Taxes (income tax), 20–44
annuities and, 66–70
"loophole" and, 21
married couples and, 22
real estate investment and, 135
state, 25
W-4 forms for withholding, 25–30, 32, 33
Tax shelters, 42–44
Tenders, 92–94
Theater tickets, 35
Treasury bills, 60–61
Treasury bonds, 61
Treasury notes, 61
Trusts, 180

Uniforms, 35

Vacation-rental property, deduction for visits to, 35
Value Line Survey, 98–99

Wallenkamp vs. *Bank of America*, 147–48
Wall Street Journal, The, 96, 116, 125–26
"Wall Street Week," 189
Weisenberger Report, 117
W-4 form, 25–30, 32, 33
Widows, 174
See also Death of a spouse
Working dollars on net worth balance sheet, 15–17